ReadyGEN®

GRADE 3

Reader's and Writer's JOURNAL

SAVVAS
LEARNING COMPANY

ISBN-13: 978-0-328-85158-4
ISBN-10:   0-328-85158-2

1 2 3 4 5 6 7 8 9 10 VON4 19 18 17 16 15

19 2020

Table of Contents

Name _____

Short Vowels and Syllables VC/CV

DIRECTIONS Choose the word with the **short vowel** sound in the **first syllable** to complete each sentence. Write the word on the line.

1. My mom works in a big (hotel/hospital). _____

2. She got the job last (April/winter). _____

3. She is a (doctor/writer). _____

4. Mom also writes (papers/letters). _____

5. She does most of her writing on a (tablet/tabletop). _____

DIRECTIONS Circle the word with the **short vowel** sound in the **first syllable**. Then underline the letter that stands for that short vowel sound.

6. happen	higher	hoses
7. miner	problem	music
8. painter	private	puppet
9. lately	lettuce	likely
10. trial	toaster	ticket
11. napkin	native	notebook
12. spoken	spider	spotlight
13. baby	blender	bleacher
14. sister	safety	season
15. guidebook	gutter	grateful

Students apply grade-level phonics and word analysis skills.

Name _____

DIRECTIONS Write a sentence using each word.

location   overtime

_____

_____

_____

_____

Write in Response to Reading

Read p. 26 from the *Text Collection*. Write several sentences that describe Evan's actions, motivations, and feelings.

_____

_____

_____

_____

_____

_____

Students demonstrate contextual understanding of Benchmark Vocabulary. Students read text closely and use text evidence in their written answers.

Name _____

Tell a Story Write a paragraph describing a story you would like to tell.

_____

_____

_____

_____

_____

_____

Conventions

Nouns

DIRECTIONS Write the nouns in the sentences.

1. Evan dragged his wagon to the center of the town.

_____

2. Evan went to the desk and worked on some problems.

_____

3. It was lunchtime and the shaded benches were filled with people.

_____

Students write routinely for a range of tasks, purposes, and audiences. Students practice various conventions of standard English.

Name _____

Benchmark Vocabulary

DIRECTIONS Write a sentence using the word.

competition

_____

_____

_____

_____

Write in Response to Reading

Read the last two paragraphs on p. 32 from the *Text Collection*. Write a paragraph that explains the sequence of events in the two paragraphs that you read. Include words and phrases that show the order of events.

_____

_____

_____

_____

_____

_____

Students demonstrate contextual understanding of Benchmark Vocabulary. Students read text closely and use text evidence in their written answers.

Name _____

Temporal Words and Phrases

DIRECTIONS Using evidence from the text, answer the following questions about "Location, Location, Location."

1. Read the second paragraph on p. 32 of "Location, Location, Location." What temporal words and phrases does the author use?

   _____

   _____

2. Explain how these words show the sequence of events.

   _____

   _____

3. Read the last two paragraphs on p. 34 of "Location, Location, Location." What temporal words and phrases does the author use?

   _____

   _____

4. What other words could the author have used to show the order of events?

   _____

   _____

Students analyze and respond to literary and informational text.

Name _____

Describe a Setting Look back at the character and problem you wrote about in Lesson 1, and decide whether they are realistic or not. Decide on an appropriate setting for your story, and write a paragraph describing it.

_____

_____

_____

_____

_____

_____

Conventions

Nouns as Subjects of Sentences

DIRECTIONS Write the subject of the following sentences:

1. But today was Friday. _____

2. His brain spun like a top. _____

3. The Jacksons went to Florida last summer. _____

Students write routinely for a range of tasks, purposes, and audiences. Students practice various conventions of standard English.

Name _____

DIRECTIONS Write a sentence using each word.

location   competition

_____

_____

_____

_____

Write in Response to Reading

Read pp. 38–39 from the *Text Collection*. What is your opinion of Evan's solution to his problem? State your opinion and support it using evidence from the text.

_____

_____

_____

_____

_____

_____

Students demonstrate contextual understanding of Benchmark Vocabulary. Students read text closely and use text evidence in their written answers.

Getting Organized

Mrs. Rodriguez asked her students to turn in their homework. Cora's stomach sank because she didn't have her homework. She remembered to do it, but she forgot to put it in her backpack. It was still sitting on the kitchen table.

"Cora," Mrs. Rodriguez said, "did you forget to do your homework again?"

"No," Cora looked down at her feet. "I did the homework, but I left it at home."

"I'm sorry to hear that, Cora," Mrs. Rodriguez said. "Bring it in tomorrow, but you will lose five points."

That night the phone rang. "Hello, Mrs. Rodriguez," Cora heard her mother answer. *This cannot be good*, Cora thought.

"Of course, I will talk to Cora."

"Cora," Mama said, "Mrs. Rodriguez says your missing and late assignments are going to affect your grade. That's a problem."

"I'm sorry," Cora said. "I'm always in such a rush in the morning. It's hard to remember everything."

"Cora, rather than being sorry," Mama said, "I want you to solve this problem. You're too smart to let a lack of organization get in the way of good grades."

"What can I do, Mama?" Cora asked.

"Let's think of some ways you can be more organized," Mama said.

Cora came up with three solutions to her problem:

1. Write down my assignments.

2. Get ready for school the night before.

3. Have Mama double-check my homework.

Three weeks later, Cora brought home her report card. Mama gave her a hug. Cora's solutions had worked!

Students read text closely to determine what the text says.

Name _____

Gather Evidence Underline 3–4 details about Cora's problem in the text on p. 8. In another color, box the 2 that are most important. Write them below.

_____

_____

_____

Gather Evidence: Extend Your Ideas Work with a partner, and discuss how changing just one of these details would affect the story.

Ask Questions Write two questions that the teacher might have asked Cora about why Cora's homework wasn't turned in on time. Bracket the words in the text that could answer the questions.

_____

Ask Questions: Extend Your Ideas Write an additional question that the teacher could have asked Cora that is answered in the text. Circle the answer in the text.

_____

Make Your Case Draw an arrow from Cora's decision (a cause) about changing her habits to what happens (the effect) at the end of the story.

Make Your Case: Extend Your Ideas Identify other causes that lead to other effects. Discuss your results with a partner.

_____

Students read text closely to determine what the text says.

Name _____

Provide Closure Write a one-paragraph narrative based on the character, problem, and setting you wrote about in Lessons 1 and 2. First, introduce your character, your setting, and the problem the character must solve. Then, add events and a solution to the problem that provides a satisfying ending to the story.

_____

_____

_____

_____

_____

Form and Use Regular Plural Nouns

DIRECTIONS Create a sentence using the plural form of each noun.

1. kid _____

2. finger _____

3. watch _____

Students write routinely for a range of tasks, purposes, and audiences. Students practice various conventions of standard English.

Name _____

DIRECTIONS Write a sentence using each word.

solution   overwhelm   efficient

_____

_____

_____

_____

Write in Response to Reading

Read pp. 2–3 of *The Case of the Gasping Garbage*. Write a short narrative from Gabby's point of view that tells what happens before she calls Drake and asks for his help. Use evidence from the text to establish the details and events.

_____

_____

_____

_____

_____

Students demonstrate contextual understanding of Benchmark Vocabulary. Students read text closely and use text evidence in their written answers.

Name _____

Introduce a Character and Setting Write a narrative paragraph that introduces a character and an interesting setting. First, introduce one character by telling the most important details the reader should know about him or her. Then introduce a setting for the character by describing the place and time clearly.

_____

_____

_____

_____

_____

_____

Identify Verbs

DIRECTIONS Read p. 3 of *The Case of the Gasping Garbage*. Find five words that are verbs, and write them on the line below.

_____

Students write routinely for a range of tasks, purposes, and audiences. Students practice various conventions of standard English.

Name _____

DIRECTIONS Write a sentence using each word.

affirmative   observations   hypothesis   mediums   culprit

_____

_____

_____

_____

_____

_____

_____

Write in Response to Reading

Read pp. 13–15 of *The Case of the Gasping Garbage*. Using evidence from the text, write an explanation of the procedure (steps) that Drake and Nell use to solve the garbage can problem.

_____

_____

_____

_____

_____

Students demonstrate contextual
understanding of Benchmark Vocabulary.
Students read text closely and use text
evidence in their written answers.

Name _____

Parts of Stories

DIRECTIONS Using evidence from the text, answer the following questions about Chapters 1 and 2 from *The Case of the Gasping Garbage*.

1. Who are the characters in Chapter 1? Who are the characters in Chapter 2?

_____

_____

_____

2. Why are some characters the same in the two chapters? Why are some characters different?

_____

_____

3. What settings are the same in both chapters?

_____

4. What are the most important events in Chapter 1? Why are they important?

_____

_____

5. What are the most important events in Chapter 2? Why are they important?

_____

_____

_____

Students analyze and respond to literary and informational text.

Name _____

Write a Character Sketch Write a character sketch of Nell Fossey that tracks her character traits, motivations, and feelings.

_____

_____

_____

_____

_____

Conventions

Form Regular Past Tense Verbs

DIRECTIONS Write the correct form of the verb on each line.

Verb	Present Tense		Past Tense
	no ending	add ending: -s	add ending: -ed
to earn	I _____	He _____	They _____
to slip	I _____	He _____	They _____
to glance	I _____	He _____	They _____

Students write routinely for a range of tasks, purposes, and audiences. Students practice various conventions of standard English.

Name _____

Plurals -s, -es, -ies

DIRECTIONS Use the plural form of each word in ( ) to complete each sentence. Write the word on the line.

1. Samuel put his hands into his (pocket). _____

2. He pulled out a handful of (penny). _____

3. He also found ten (dollar). _____

4. He used the money to buy three (paintbrush). _____

5. Later, Samuel squeezed paint from several (tube). _____

6. He sketched a row of (box). _____

7. In each one, he painted five (pansy). _____

8. Each pansy had five (petal). _____

9. The finished painting measured 48 (inch). _____

10. Samuel gave it to his two best (friend). _____

DIRECTIONS Write the plural form of each word.

11. lady _____   16. supply _____

12. dish _____   17. wax _____

13. glass _____   18. itch _____

14. pose _____   19. daisy _____

15. book _____   20. rock _____

Students apply grade-level phonics and word analysis skills.

Name _____

DIRECTIONS Write a sentence using each word.

confirmed   naturalist

_____

_____

_____

_____

Write in Response to Reading

Read the fourth paragraph on p. 20 of *The Case of the Gasping Garbage*. The narrator makes statements about Nell Fossey. Do you agree with these statements? State your opinion and support it using text evidence.

_____

_____

_____

_____

_____

_____

Students demonstrate contextual understanding of Benchmark Vocabulary. Students read text closely and use text evidence in their written answers.

Name _____

Establish a Situation Continue with the narrative you began in Lesson 4 by describing an event that introduces a problem.

_____

_____

_____

_____

_____

_____

Conventions

Form and Use Simple Verb Tenses

DIRECTIONS Form the past tense, present tense, and future tense of the following verbs:

1. talk _____

2. jump _____

3. crawl _____

Students write routinely for a range of tasks, purposes, and audiences. Students practice various conventions of standard English.

Name _____

DIRECTIONS Write a sentence using each word.

pollution   habitat

_____

_____

_____

_____

Write in Response to Reading

How would you describe Drake's and Nell's motivations and actions? What do they do to show motivation? Use an example from the text to support your answer.

_____

_____

_____

_____

_____

_____

Students demonstrate contextual understanding of Benchmark Vocabulary. Students read text closely and use text evidence in their written answers.

Name _____

Write a Series of Events in Order Continue with the narrative you began in Lessons 4 and 6 by writing a series of events that seem to unfold naturally. First, list a series of events. Then, put them in a logical order.

_____

_____

_____

_____

_____

Form Simple Sentences Using Regular Verbs

DIRECTIONS Write two simple sentences that use regular verbs.

_____

_____

_____

Students write routinely for a range of tasks, purposes, and audiences. Students practice various conventions of standard English.

Name _____

DIRECTIONS Write a sentence using each word.

desperate   situation   stumped   archrival   analysis

_____

_____

_____

_____

_____

_____

Write in Response to Reading

Read the paragraph on p. 32 of *The Case of the Gasping Garbage* that begins "This is a chance for Doyle and Fossey." Write a brief narrative in which you retell this part of the story from Frisco's perspective.

_____

_____

_____

_____

_____

Students demonstrate contextual understanding of Benchmark Vocabulary. Students read text closely and use text evidence in their written answers.

Name _____

Sequence of Events

DIRECTIONS Using evidence from the text, answer the following questions about Chapter 5 from *The Case of the Gasping Garbage.*

1. What is the sequence, or order, of events?

   _____

   _____

   _____

   _____

2. What does Nell do to affect these events? What does Drake do to affect these events?

   _____

   _____

   _____

3. Compare and contrast the effect of Drake's actions and Nell's actions on the sequence of events.

   _____

   _____

   _____

   _____

4. What are the most important events in Chapter 5? Why are they important?

   _____

   _____

   _____

   _____

Students analyze and respond to literary and informational text.

Name _____

Use Temporal Words and Phrases Write a one-paragraph narrative using the events you listed in Lesson 7. Use temporal (time order) words or phrases to begin the event sequence, to signal the order of events, and to end the event sequence.

_____

_____

_____

_____

_____

Conventions

Form Simple Sentences with Nouns, Verbs, and Temporal Words

DIRECTIONS Form three simple sentences using a noun, a verb, and a temporal word or phrase.

_____

_____

_____

_____

_____

Students write routinely for a range of tasks, purposes, and audiences. Students practice various conventions of standard English.

Name _____

DIRECTIONS Write a sentence using each word.

surveyed   deflate

_____

_____

_____

_____

Write in Response to Reading

Read the third paragraph on p. 43 of *The Case of the Gasping Garbage*.
The narrator states that Nell's tadpoles were glad to see her. Describe
Nell's experience when she finally got home.

_____

_____

_____

_____

_____

Students demonstrate contextual
understanding of Benchmark Vocabulary.
Students read text closely and use text
evidence in their written answers.

Name _____

Write a Dialogue Write a dialogue between two characters that develops their experiences. Make sure the dialogue sounds like two real people are talking.

_____

_____

_____

_____

_____

Conventions

Use Quotation Marks in Dialogue

DIRECTIONS Use quotation marks to separate the dialogue from the description.

1. Where did you get that from? asked Joe.

2. Mother said, I want you to come home for dinner.

3. Don't forget your scarf! yelled Lauren.

 Students write routinely for a range of tasks, purposes, and audiences. Students practice various conventions of standard English.

Name _____

DIRECTIONS Write a sentence using each word.

anonymous   suspended

_____

_____

_____

Write in Response to Reading

Read p. 50 of *The Case of the Gasping Garbage.* How might you have gone about your investigation differently than Drake and Nell went about their investigation? State your opinion and support it using text evidence.

_____

_____

_____

_____

_____

_____

Students demonstrate contextual understanding of Benchmark Vocabulary. Students read text closely and use text evidence in their written answers.

Name _____

Point of View

DIRECTIONS Using evidence from the text, answer the following questions about p. 45 from *The Case of the Gasping Garbage.*

1. What is Drake's point of view about cases involving love?

   _____

   _____

2. Would you take a case that involves love? Explain your answer.

   _____

   _____

3. How does Lilly feel about finding the person who wrote her a love letter?

   _____

   _____

4. What evidence supports your answer?

   _____

   _____

   _____

5. How would you feel about finding the person who wrote you a love letter? Explain your answer.

   _____

   _____

Students analyze and respond to literary and informational text.

Name _____

Write a Dialogue For one of the characters in the narrative you have been working on, write a dialogue that reveals his or her response to a situation.

_____

_____

_____

_____

_____

_____

Conventions

Use Commas in Dialogue

DIRECTIONS Insert commas into the dialogue.

1. "I am tired" Evan said.

2. The detective thought "I can solve anything!"

3. "Let's go to the mall" replied Debra.

Students write routinely for a range of tasks, purposes, and audiences. Students practice various conventions of standard English.

Name _____

Base Words and Endings

DIRECTIONS Add *-ed* and *-ing* to each word on the left. Remember that you may have to double the last consonant or drop the final *e*.

Word	-ed	-ing
plan	planned	planning
1. please	_____	_____
2. close	_____	_____
3. shop	_____	_____
4. tire	_____	_____
5. tug	_____	_____

DIRECTIONS Add *-er* and *-est* to each word on the left. Remember that you may have to double the last consonant, drop the final *e*, or change *y* to *i*.

Word	-er	-est
heavy	heavier	heaviest
6. soft	_____	_____
7. easy	_____	_____
8. thin	_____	_____
9. fluffy	_____	_____
10. sore	_____	_____

Students apply grade-level phonics and word analysis skills.

Name _____

DIRECTIONS Write a sentence using the word.

elementary

_____

_____

_____

Write in Response to Reading

Skim through Chapter 8 of *The Case of the Gasping Garbage* to remind yourself of its main points. On a separate sheet of paper, write a short narrative that describes what Lilly does after she finds out who wrote the love letter. Keep in mind that characters' actions impact the sequence of events in a story.

_____

_____

_____

_____

_____

Students demonstrate contextual understanding of Benchmark Vocabulary. Students read text closely and use text evidence in their written answers.

Name _____

Use Description to Develop Experiences Write a narrative that uses description to develop a character's experience. Describe an action, a thought, or a feeling using descriptive details.

_____

_____

_____

_____

_____

_____

How Nouns Function in a Sentence

DIRECTIONS Circle the subject, and underline the direct object in each sentence.

1. The batter hit the ball.

2. The man built a house.

3. The dog is eating its food.

Students write routinely for a range of tasks, purposes, and audiences. Students practice various conventions of standard English.

Name _____

DIRECTIONS Write a sentence using each word.

solution   observations   hypothesis

_____

_____

_____

_____

Write in Response to Reading

Read pp. 16–17 in *The Case of the Gasping Garbage* and pp. 37–39 in "Location, Location, Location." Compare and contrast the way Drake, Nell, and Evan identify problems and find solutions. Support your answers using text evidence.

_____

_____

_____

_____

_____

Students demonstrate contextual understanding of Benchmark Vocabulary. Students read text closely and use text evidence in their written answers.

Name _____

Sequence of Events

DIRECTIONS Using evidence from the text, answer the following questions about *The Case of the Gasping Garbage* and "Location, Location, Location."

1. In "Location, Location, Location," what decision does Evan make after he hears how much the lemonade costs in the ice cream shop? What happens after he makes this decision?

   _____

   _____

2. What happens to Evan's lemonade stand because of his decision to sell lemonade in the town center?

   _____

   _____

   _____

3. In *The Case of the Gasping Garbage*, how does Drake respond when Gabby threatens to call Frisco? Why does he respond this way?

   _____

   _____

   _____

4. Why does Drake decide not to open Gabby's garbage can? What do Drake and Nell do instead to help them solve the case?

   _____

   _____

   _____

Students analyze and respond to literary and informational text.

Name _____

Use Description to Show Responses Write a paragraph that describes the response of a character to a situation. Conclude with a sentence describing what will happen next.

_____

_____

_____

_____

_____

_____

Form and Use Irregular Plural Nouns

DIRECTIONS Use the plural of each noun in a sentence.

1. foot _____

2. man _____

3. leaf _____

4. mouse _____

5. child _____

Students write routinely for a range of tasks, purposes, and audiences. Students practice various conventions of standard English.

Name _____

DIRECTIONS Write a sentence using each word.

overcome   horizon   squinted   luscious

_____

_____

_____

_____

_____

Write in Response to Reading

Read p. 12 of *Thunder Cake.* The narrator says she was scared while walking through Tangleweed Woods to collect the ingredients from the dry shed. Why do you think she was scared? State your opinion and support it using text evidence.

_____

_____

_____

_____

_____

Students demonstrate contextual
understanding of Benchmark Vocabulary.
Students read text closely and use text
evidence in their written answers.

Name _____

Lin's Lesson

"You know you're not supposed to bring food downstairs," Mom said to Lin. She was walking up the stairs from Lin's bedroom holding a plate of dried-up sandwich. "When you leave food out, bugs come, and I can't stand bugs. If you want a snack, eat it upstairs."

"Yes, Mom," Lin said, only half paying attention. He didn't see what the big deal was and why she was so worried about bugs. The few he'd seen in his room were harmless little ants. Sometimes when he was drawing, he got so preoccupied that he forgot about the snacks he had brought downstairs.

The next morning, Lin woke up to a strange sensation. He opened his eyes and saw ants crawling over his arm. Lin bolted out of bed. Ants were crawling on the floor and in and out of the pretzel bag that was open on his desk. Lin ran upstairs, where he found his mom drinking her morning cup of tea.

"Mom!" Lin howled. "There are ants all over my room, even in my bed! I never thought this would happen!"

"Oh, Lin," Mom replied, "that's why we have rules—to avoid just this kind of thing. I'll have to call the exterminator, and you'll have to save your allowance and pay me back. Got it?"

"Yes, Mom. I'm really sorry." Lin had learned his lesson the hard way! He would have to use his own money to pay to get the ants removed.

Students read text closely to determine what the text says.

Name _____

Gather Evidence Circle 3 details from "Lin's Lesson" to support whether or not Lin learns his lesson. In another color, circle the detail that best supports whether Lin learns his lesson.

Gather Evidence: Extend Your Ideas Briefly explain why the circled details are important to the story. Then work with a partner, and discuss how changing just one of these details would affect the story.

_____

Ask Questions Write two questions you think Lin and his mother would ask each other about this experience a week after it happened. Underline any words that could help answer the first question. Underline twice any words that could help answer the second question.

_____

_____

Ask Questions: Extend Your Ideas Did you underline any answers in the text? If the answer is yes, explain. If the answer is no, write another question that the text answers and the answer from the text below.

_____

_____

Make Your Case Choose either Lin or his mother. Circle 3–4 details the writer includes to show how the character feels.

Make Your Case: Extend Your Ideas Write 1–2 sentences explaining how essential Lin's or his mother's feelings are to the story. How would the story be different if their feelings were exchanged?

_____

_____

Students read text closely to determine what the text says.

Name _____

Provide a Sense of Closure On a separate sheet of paper, write a brief narrative that introduces a character and a problem, explains the character's solution to the problem, and provides a sense of closure.

Identify the Functions of Verbs

DIRECTIONS Identify the verb and function of the verb in the following sentences:

1. The man was tall. _____

2. Grandma looked at the horizon. _____

3. Kelly walks to the store every week. _____

Students write routinely for a range of tasks, purposes, and audiences. Students practice various conventions of standard English.

Benchmark Vocabulary

Name _____

DIRECTIONS Write a sentence using each word.

overcome   horizon

_____

_____

_____

_____

Write in Response to Reading

Read p. 5 of *Thunder Cake*. This introduction is told from the granddaughter's point of view. Retell the introduction to *Thunder Cake* from Grandma's point of view.

_____

_____

_____

_____

_____

_____

Students demonstrate contextual understanding of Benchmark Vocabulary. Students read text closely and use text evidence in their written answers.

Name _____

Words That Create Effect

DIRECTIONS Using evidence from the text, answer the following questions about *Thunder Cake*.

1. Read p. 5 of *Thunder Cake*. What are some words the author uses to describe the characters or setting?

   _____

   _____

2. Explain how the author uses these descriptive details to develop the setting.

   _____

   _____

3. What effect do these details have on the story?

   _____

   _____

4. Read the sentences on p. 17 of *Thunder Cake*. How does the author use descriptive details to develop Grandma's character?

   _____

   _____

5. What effect do these words and phrases have on the story?

   _____

   _____

Students analyze and respond to literary and informational text.

Name _____

Plan and Prewrite Plan a story similar to *Thunder Cake* in which you write about a time when fear turned into courage.

_____

_____

_____

_____

_____

Conventions

Identify Forms of Irregular Verbs

DIRECTIONS Underline the irregular verb in each sentence.

1. Florence walked back to her house because she had forgotten her bag.

2. Wallace understood that he could not talk loudly in the library.

3. Gloria fixed the flat tire and drove home.

Students write routinely for a range of tasks, purposes, and audiences. Students practice various conventions of standard English.

Name _____

DIRECTIONS Write a sentence using each word.

squinted   luscious

_____

_____

_____

_____

Write in Response to Reading

Read pp. 5–8 of *Thunder Cake*. Write a sentence or two explaining why Grandma chose to bake a Thunder Cake. Use text evidence to support your explanation.

_____

_____

_____

_____

_____

Students demonstrate contextual understanding of Benchmark Vocabulary. Students read text closely and use text evidence in their written answers.

Name _____

Draft Draft the story you planned in Lesson 14 on a separate sheet of paper.

Verbs That End in -y

DIRECTIONS Rewrite the following sentences using the verbs in the past tense:

1. Nell hurries to campus. _____

2. The pirates bury treasure. _____

3. Gregory will study for the test. _____

Students write routinely for a range of tasks, purposes, and audiences. Students practice various conventions of standard English.

Name _____

Vowel Digraphs *ee, ea, ai, ay, oa, ow*

DIRECTIONS Choose the word with the **long a, long e,** or **long o** sound that best matches each definition. Write the word on the line.

1. all right   _____   glad   okay   well

2. winter garment   _____   hat   boot   coat

3. free of dirt   _____   clean   fresh   spotless

4. toss   _____   pitch   lob   throw

5. go along   _____   admit   agree   settle

6. lift up   _____   raise   heft   build

7. warm up   _____   cook   toast   broil

8. remain   _____   stay   last   linger

9. type of grass   _____   moss   reed   straw

DIRECTIONS Circle the word that has the **long a, long e,** or **long o** sound. Then underline the letters in the word that stand for that vowel sound.

10. crop   clock   creek

11. belt   below   bought

12. latch   float   bread

13. braid   bride   brook

14. feast   flash   frost

15. stray   struck   stop

Students apply grade-level phonics and word analysis skills.

Name _____

DIRECTIONS Write a sentence using each word.

observations   situation

_____

_____

_____

_____

Write in Response to Reading

Read p. 18 in *The Case of the Gasping Garbage* from "It was Friday after school . . . " to "Mrs. Doyle closed the door." Then read pp. 6–7 in *Thunder Cake* from "'Steady child . . . '" to "'Thunder Cake?' I stammered as I hugged her even closer." Which text do you think uses narrative techniques more effectively? State your opinion. Then support your opinion with reasons and evidence from the text.

_____

_____

_____

_____

_____

Students demonstrate contextual understanding of Benchmark Vocabulary. Students read text closely and use text evidence in their written answers.

Name _____

Revise On a separate sheet of paper, revise the narrative you drafted in Lesson 15. Look for areas where you can add details and descriptive language to make your story more interesting and areas where you can add appropriate dialogue. Make sure that the end resolves the problem in your story.

Conventions

Use Irregular Verbs in Sentences

DIRECTIONS For each verb below, write one sentence that uses the verb in the present tense, one sentence that uses the verb in the past tense, and one sentence that uses the verb's past participle.

1. become

_____

_____

_____

2. shake

_____

_____

_____

Students write routinely for a range of tasks, purposes, and audiences. Students practice various conventions of standard English.

Name _____

DIRECTIONS Write a sentence using each word.

location   earned   competition

_____

_____

_____

_____

Write in Response to Reading

Read p. 31 from "He needed a plan" to "He just needed to find something with wheels to get him there" in "Location, Location, Location." Then read pp. 6–7 of *Thunder Cake* from "The air was hot, heavy and damp" to "'Thunder Cake?' I stammered as I hugged her even closer." Compare and contrast the way Grandma and Evan identify problems and find solutions. Support your answers using text evidence.

_____

_____

_____

_____

_____

Students demonstrate contextual understanding of Benchmark Vocabulary. Students read text closely and use text evidence in their written answers.

Name _____

Compare Narratives

DIRECTIONS Using evidence from the texts, answer the following questions about "Location, Location, Location" and *Thunder Cake*.

1. Describe how Evan identifies problems and finds solutions.

   _____

   _____

2. Describe how Grandma identifies problems and finds solutions.

   _____

   _____

3. How is Evan's process for identifying problems and finding solutions different from Grandma's process?

   _____

   _____

4. How is it similar to Grandma's process?

   _____

   _____

Students analyze and respond to literary and informational text.

Name _____

Edit Edit the story you began in Lesson 14. Write your edited story on a separate sheet of paper.

Conventions

Identify Pronouns

DIRECTIONS Underline the pronoun in each sentence.

1. Drake couldn't believe them.

2. He wanted to find a way for the frogs to cross the street safely.

3. She said the bandage was too tight.

Students write routinely for a range of tasks, purposes, and audiences. Students practice various conventions of standard English.

Name _____

DIRECTIONS Write a sentence using each word.

anonymous   elementary

_____

_____

_____

_____

Write in Response to Reading

Read p. 18 in *The Case of the Gasping Garbage* from "It was Friday after school . . ." to "Mrs. Doyle closed the door." Then read p. 18 in *Thunder Cake* from "But you got out from under it" to "'From where I sit, only a very brave person could have done all them things!'" Finally, read p. 31 in "Location, Location, Location" from "It took Evan half an hour to drag his loaded wagon to the town center" to "But once he was there, he knew it was worth it." Compare and contrast the way in which one character from each text changes over time. Support your answers using text evidence.

_____

_____

_____

_____

_____

Students demonstrate contextual understanding of Benchmark Vocabulary. Students read text closely and use text evidence in their written answers.

Publish and Present Publish and present your narrative. Write the final version of your narrative on a separate sheet of paper.

Using Pronouns in Sentences

DIRECTIONS Circle the nouns in each sentence. Then write a pronoun that could replace each noun on the line below the sentence.

1. Drake and Nell can solve a problem by working in the lab or talking with friends.

   _____

2. Grandma whispered as she squinted at the list.

   _____

3. Evan decided to draw dollar signs.

   _____

Students write routinely for a range of tasks, purposes, and audiences. Students practice various conventions of standard English.

Vowel Digraphs ee, ea, ai, ay, oa, ow

DIRECTIONS Use context to help you complete each sentence with one or more words from the Word Bank. You will not use all of the words.

Word Bank

steal	float	rays	thrown	knees	shadow
coach	reached	lower	brain	away	between
straight	trait	feet	stay	road	bleachers

1. I saw that the catcher had _____ the ball to third base.

2. I decided to try to _____ second base.

3. The ball seemed to _____ slowly through the air.

4. My _____ yelled for me to _____ on first.

5. However, I had already stepped _____ from the base.

6. My _____ had already told my legs to run, so I went.

7. The fans in the _____ yelled for me to run.

8. I was still _____ bases when my _____ got tangled.

9. I was lucky—the catcher's throw went _____ into the stands!

10. I _____ third base, where I was safe.

11. I fell to my _____ with relief.

12. The _____ of bright sunlight must have blinded her.

DIRECTIONS Combine each word on the left with the word on the right that has the same long vowel sound. Write the new word on the line.

13. _____   rail   boat

14. _____   sea   way

15. _____   show   weed

Students apply grade-level phonics and word analysis skills.

Benchmark Vocabulary

Name _____

DIRECTIONS Write a sentence using each word.

quarter   crescent   waxing   waning   phases

_____

_____

_____

_____

_____

_____

_____

Write in Response to Reading

Read p. 43 from *The Moon Seems to Change* and study the illustrations. According to the text, "the moon seems to change." How does the moon's appearance change over time?

_____

_____

_____

_____

_____

Students demonstrate contextual understanding of Benchmark Vocabulary. Students read text closely and use text evidence in their written answers.

Name _____

Convey Ideas and Information Write a paragraph that introduces a topic and uses facts to explain it. First, write a sentence that introduces and explains your topic. Then, list three facts and key details that support your topic.

_____

_____

_____

_____

_____

Conventions

Nouns as Subjects

DIRECTIONS Underline the noun that serves as the subject of each sentence.

1. Each night the crescent gets a bit thinner.

2. Spaceships went around the moon.

3. The sky is dark.

Students write routinely for a range of tasks, purposes, and audiences. Students practice various conventions of standard English.

Name _____

DIRECTIONS Write a sentence using each word.

waxing   waning

_____

_____

_____

_____

Write in Response to Reading

Read p. 55 from *The Moon Seems to Change*. Write a paragraph explaining how the phases of the moon cause the moon to seem to change. Be sure to support your explanation using details from the text.

_____

_____

_____

_____

_____

_____

_____

_____

Students demonstrate contextual understanding of Benchmark Vocabulary. Students read text closely and use text evidence in their written answers.

Name _____

Text Features

DIRECTIONS Using evidence from the text, answer the following questions about pp. 46–53 of *The Moon Seems to Change*.

1. Look at the illustrations at the bottom of p. 48. What do they show?

   _____

   _____

2. How do they help the reader understand why the moon only *seems* to change?

   _____

   _____

   _____

3. Look at the illustration at the bottom of p. 49. What does it show?

   _____

   _____

4. How does it help the reader understand why the moon only *seems* to change?

   _____

   _____

   _____

Students analyze and respond to literary and informational text.

Name _____

Genre Write a paragraph that identifies the genre of the paragraph you wrote in Lesson 1 and explains the reasons you used to identify the paragraph's genre.

_____

_____

_____

_____

_____

_____

Use a Noun as a Subject

DIRECTIONS For each noun below, write a sentence that uses the noun as a subject.

1. planet _____

2. star _____

3. day _____

Students write routinely for a range of tasks, purposes, and audiences. Students practice various conventions of standard English.

Name _____

DIRECTIONS Write a sentence using each word.

quarter   crescent   phases

_____

_____

_____

_____

Write in Response to Reading

Read p. 50 of *The Moon Seems to Change*. Look at the illustrations and write about what you see. How do the illustrations help you understand the text? Support your response with evidence from the text.

_____

_____

_____

_____

_____

Students demonstrate contextual understanding of Benchmark Vocabulary. Students read text closely and use text evidence in their written answers.

Name _____

A Whale of a Rescue

Imagine walking along the beach and stopping now and then to pick up an interesting shell. You see something at the water's edge. You realize it's a whale—a whale stranded on the beach.

Some animals, such as seals, often come out of the water onto the shore. But for whales, dolphins, and porpoises, this behavior usually means that something is wrong. Sometimes the animal is sick, but sometimes it has just lost its way. Swimming in stormy seas can exhaust some animals. Their exhaustion will make them disoriented. Others get stuck in shallow waters when the tide is outgoing.

One time, in February 2011, not just one whale, but 82 were stranded! For reasons unknown, 82 pilot whales became stranded on a beach in New Zealand.

The Department of Conservation of New Zealand, along with over 100 volunteers, came to the rescue. They worked all weekend long to get the animals back into the water. All but 17 whales made it.

Then, just days later, 65 whales were stranded again! This time, the volunteers didn't try to move the whales back into the water. "New evidence suggests that moving stranded whales causes them a lot of stress and pain," Department of Conservation ranger Simon Walls told a local newspaper. Instead, the volunteers cared for the whales on shore while waiting for the high tides to return.

All 65 of the newly stranded whales were successfully returned to the water. The plan had worked!

Students read text closely to determine what the text says.

Gather Evidence Underline 3–4 details in the text that explain why whales might become stranded on the beach.

Gather Evidence: Extend Your Ideas Work with a partner, and discuss how changing just one of these details would affect the text.

Ask Questions Write three questions about the stranded pilot whales and the people who tried to help them. Highlight words in the text that could help answer your first question. Bracket any words that could help answer your second question. Draw a box around any words that could help answer your third question.

_____

_____

_____

Ask Questions: Extend Your Ideas Did you mark any words in the text that would answer your questions? If the answer is yes, explain. If the answer is no, write another question that the text answers and the answer from the text below.

_____

_____

Make Your Case Circle words in the text that the author uses to compare and contrast the two events in the text.

Make Your Case: Extend Your Ideas Write 2–3 sentences comparing and contrasting the two events.

_____

Students read text closely to determine what the text says.

Name _____

Use Illustrations to Convey Information Review the paragraph you wrote for Lesson 1. Decide which fact or facts could be better explained in an illustration or diagram. Draw the illustration or diagram below or on a separate sheet of paper.

Conventions

Subject-Verb Agreement: Past Tense

DIRECTIONS Write the correct past-tense form of the verb *be* in each sentence.

1. The cows _____ hungry.

2. I _____ very tired last night.

3. You _____ my best friend.

 Students write routinely for a range of tasks, purposes, and audiences. Students practice various conventions of standard English.

Name _____

DIRECTIONS Write a sentence using each word.

gnarled   scowls

_____

_____

_____

Write in Response to Reading

Read p. 8 of *Treasure in the Trees*. How do Nisha's parents view the success of their shop? How do you view the success of their shop? Support your answer with evidence from the text.

_____

_____

_____

_____

_____

Students demonstrate contextual understanding of Benchmark Vocabulary. Students read text closely and use text evidence in their written answers.

Name _____

Point of View

DIRECTIONS Using evidence from the text, answer the following questions about pp. 6–7 of *Treasure in the Trees*.

1. How do Nisha's parents feel about her changing an image of her grandparents? What evidence from the text supports your answer?

_____

_____

_____

_____

2. How do you feel about Nisha changing an image of her grandparents?

_____

_____

3. How does Nisha feel about convincing her parents to save the tree? What evidence from the text supports your answer?

_____

_____

_____

_____

4. How do you think Nisha should feel about convincing her parents to save the tree?

_____

_____

Students analyze and respond to literary and informational text.

Name _____

Introduce a Topic Decide what the topic and main idea of your informative/explanatory text will be. Then write one or two sentences that introduce the topic and one or two sentences that state your main idea.

_____

_____

_____

_____

_____

Subject-Verb Agreement: Past Tense

DIRECTIONS Complete each sentence with the past-tense form of the verb.

1. Tina _____ (decide) to tell her best friend her secret.

2. Her parents _____ (be) always tired after working at the hotel.

3. We _____ (play) with our turtle, Scooter.

Students write routinely for a range of tasks, purposes, and audiences. Students practice various conventions of standard English.

Name _____

DIRECTIONS Write a sentence using each word.

exasperated   grove   frustrated   underside

_____

_____

_____

_____

_____

_____

_____

_____

_____

Write in Response to Reading

Reread the last paragraph on p. 13. How does the sentence structure help communicate a change in Nisha's attention?

_____

_____

_____

_____

_____

Students demonstrate contextual understanding of Benchmark Vocabulary. Students read text closely and use text evidence in their written answers.

Name _____

Group Related Information Reread the introductory paragraph you wrote in Lesson 4. Gather and group information related to your topic. Then write it below. Look for ways the groups of information can suggest sub-ideas or key details for your essay.

_____

_____

_____

_____

_____

_____

Produce Simple Sentences

DIRECTIONS Write three simple sentences. One sentence should have two subjects, and one sentence should have two verbs.

_____

_____

_____

Students write routinely for a range of tasks, purposes, and audiences. Students practice various conventions of standard English.

Name _____

Vowel Diphthongs *ou, ow, oi, oy*

DIRECTIONS Circle each word with **ou** or **ow** that has the same vowel sound as **out**. Then write the word or words on the line.

_____ **1.** Jen slowly counted her money.

_____ **2.** She had the amount she needed.

_____ **3.** Jen was proud that she had earned enough.

_____ **4.** Now she could buy flowers for her mother's show.

_____ **5.** "Good going!" she said aloud.

DIRECTIONS Circle each word with **oi** or **oy** that has the same vowel sound as **toy**. Then write the word or words on the line.

_____ **6.** It was time for Ivan to make a choice.

_____ **7.** Should he find a new employer?

_____ **8.** Here, the noise really annoyed him.

_____ **9.** He just wanted to enjoy his job.

_____ **10.** His noisy coworkers spoiled everything.

DIRECTIONS Circle each word with the same vowel sound as the first word. Then underline the letters in the circled word that stand for that vowel sound.

11. town	loyal	proud	snow
12. joy	sound	know	broil
13. voice	vote	plow	soil
14. hour	crown	float	show
15. join	bay	annoy	brown

Students apply grade-level phonics and word analysis skills.

Name _____

DIRECTIONS Write a sentence using each word.

urged   creature   destroyed

_____

_____

_____

_____

_____

_____

Write in Response to Reading

Read p. 15 of *Treasure in the Trees*. How have Nisha's parents changed?
Use evidence from the text to support your answer.

_____

_____

_____

_____

_____

_____

Students demonstrate contextual
understanding of Benchmark Vocabulary.
Students read text closely and use text
evidence in their written answers.

Name _____

Analyze Character

DIRECTIONS Using evidence from the text, answer the following questions about pp. 18–19 of *Treasure in the Trees*.

1. What does Nisha's father think of her observation about the curled leaves in the tree?

    _____

    _____

2. What evidence from the text supports your answer?

    _____

    _____

    _____

    _____

3. How does Nisha feel about her parents' response to seeing the curled leaves in the tree?

    _____

    _____

4. What evidence from the text supports your answer?

    _____

    _____

Students analyze and respond to literary and informational text.

Name _____

Use Linking Words and Phrases to Connect Ideas On a separate sheet of paper, write several paragraphs that organize and develop the related ideas and details you grouped in Lesson 5. Use linking words and phrases to connect the ideas and details in your paragraphs.

Conventions

Subject-Verb Agreement: Present Tense

DIRECTIONS Fill in each blank with the present-tense form of the verb that agrees with the subject of the sentence.

1. Crystal's dog _____ (be) small.

2. Her grandmother _____ (cook) dinner.

3. "We _____ (be) very tired," her mother said.

Students write routinely for a range of tasks, purposes, and audiences. Students practice various conventions of standard English.

Name _____

DIRECTIONS Write a sentence using each word.

unfurled   hastily   rumbling   desperately

_____
_____
_____
_____
_____

Write in Response to Reading

Look at the illustration on p. 20 of *Treasure in the Trees*. What details from the text does the illustration show? How does it contribute to the story?

_____
_____
_____
_____
_____

Students demonstrate contextual understanding of Benchmark Vocabulary. Students read text closely and use text evidence in their written answers.

Use Linking Words and Phrases to Compare Ideas On a separate sheet of paper, write several paragraphs that organize and develop the related ideas you grouped in Lesson 5. Use linking words and phrases to connect the ideas by comparing and contrasting them.

Conventions

Subject-Verb Agreement: Present Tense

DIRECTIONS Complete each sentence with the present-tense form of the verb.

1. Theresa _____ (worry) about her little brother.

2. It _____ (glide) through the water.

3. He _____ (watch) the phone fall out of her pocket.

Students write routinely for a range of tasks, purposes, and audiences. Students practice various conventions of standard English.

Name _____

DIRECTIONS Write a sentence using each word.

inched   exclaimed   creatures   generous   triumphantly

_____

_____

_____

_____

_____

_____

_____

Write in Response to Reading

Read p. 31 of *Treasure in the Trees*. How do Nisha's parents respond when she shows them her notebook? Why do you think they respond this way? Use text evidence to support your answer.

_____

_____

_____

_____

_____

Students demonstrate contextual understanding of Benchmark Vocabulary. Students read text closely and use text evidence in their written answers.

Name _____

Identifying and Explaining Key Events

DIRECTIONS Using evidence from the text, answer the following questions about pp. 30–33 of *Treasure in the Trees*.

1. What key event happens on p. 30? Why is this event important?

_____

_____

_____

2. What two key events happen on p. 31? Why are they important?

_____

_____

_____

_____

3. How do these two events affect Nisha's actions?

_____

_____

_____

4. What key event happens on p. 33? Why is this event important?

_____

_____

_____

_____

Students analyze and respond to literary and informational text.

Name _____

Develop the Topic Review the paragraphs you wrote in Lessons 6 and 7, looking for ideas that need more supporting facts or explanatory details and for unfamiliar terms that need to be defined. On a separate sheet of paper, add facts, definitions, and details to the paragraphs where needed.

Conventions

Subject-Verb Agreement: Future Tense

DIRECTIONS Complete each sentence with the future tense of the verb.

1. I _____ (run) a mile tonight.

2. The teacher _____ (give) us our assignment tomorrow.

3. His friends _____ (plan) a birthday party for him.

Students write routinely for a range of tasks, purposes, and audiences. Students practice various conventions of standard English.

Name _____

DIRECTIONS Write a sentence using each word.

fascinated   unison   amazing   embraced

_____

_____

_____

_____

_____

_____

Write in Response to Reading

What lesson do you think Nisha's parents learn in Chapter 6 of *Treasure in the Trees*? Use evidence from the text to support your answer.

_____

_____

_____

_____

_____

_____

Students demonstrate contextual understanding of Benchmark Vocabulary. Students read text closely and use text evidence in their written answers.

Name _____

Draw an Illustration Look at your list of illustrations that might help you communicate the main ideas and key details in the piece of writing you began in Lesson 4. Draw one of those illustrations below or on a separate sheet of paper.

Conventions

Produce Simple Sentences Using Subject-Verb Agreement: Future Tense

DIRECTIONS Write two simple sentences, each with a verb in the future tense and correct subject-verb agreement.

_____

_____

Students write routinely for a range of tasks, purposes, and audiences. Students practice various conventions of standard English.

Name _____

DIRECTIONS Write a sentence using each word.

planet　　　liquid　　　surrounds

_____

_____

_____

_____

Write in Response to Reading

Look at the photo of the astronaut on p. 5. How does it help you better understand gravity on Earth's moon?

_____

_____

_____

_____

_____

Students demonstrate contextual understanding of Benchmark Vocabulary. Students read text closely and use text evidence in their written answers.

Name _____

Write a Concluding Statement or Section Review the main ideas and supporting details in the piece of informative/explanatory writing that you began in Lesson 4. Think about the following questions:

1. What is interesting or important about your main idea?

2. Why would someone want or need to know about it?

3. Why does the topic of your essay matter?

Use your answers to these questions to help you write a concluding statement or section on a separate sheet of paper.

Conventions

Use Adjectives

DIRECTIONS Underline the adjective(s) in each sentence.

1. The huge bowl held sour candy.

2. My lazy cat likes to sleep on my soft blanket.

3. None of Delilah's tall friends like to ride in her small car.

Students write routinely for a range of tasks, purposes, and audiences. Students practice various conventions of standard English.

Name _____

Syllable Patterns V/CV, VC/V

DIRECTIONS Circle each word in the box with the **long vowel** sound in the **first syllable**. Underline each word in the box with the **short vowel** sound in the **first syllable**. Then write each word in the correct column.

gravy	seven	finish	lady	robot
panel	viper	credit	modern	weasel

long vowel

1. _____
2. _____
3. _____
4. _____
5. _____

short vowel

6. _____
7. _____
8. _____
9. _____
10. _____

DIRECTIONS Cross out the words in the Word Bank that have a **short vowel** sound in the **first syllable**. Then complete the sentences with the words that have a **long vowel** sound in the **first syllable**.

Word Bank

cousin	chosen	pleasant	tiny	menu
raisins	honest	pupils	camels	reason

11. The normally quiet _____ began to shout.

12. Their teacher tried to figure out the _____.

13. He learned it once a spokesperson had been _____.

14. The students were upset about _____ dots in the cereal.

15. None of them had ever seen _____ before!

Students apply grade-level phonics and word analysis skills.

Name _____

DIRECTIONS Write a sentence using each word.

oceans   contain   streams

_____

_____

_____

_____

Write in Response to Reading

Why is the amount of water humans can drink limited even though 70% of Earth's surface is covered in water?

_____

_____

_____

_____

_____

Students demonstrate contextual understanding of Benchmark Vocabulary. Students read text closely and use text evidence in their written answers.

Name _____

Main Idea and Key Details

DIRECTIONS   Using evidence from the text, answer the following questions about pp. 6–11 from *About Earth*.

1. How are lakes and oceans similar?

   _____

   _____

2. How are lakes and oceans different?

   _____

   _____

3. What would happen if all the ice on Earth melted? What does this tell you about Earth's water?

   _____

   _____

   _____

4. Where can you find fresh water?

   _____

   _____

Students analyze and respond to literary and informational text.

Name _____

Present Review the written version of your informative/explanatory report. Write a paragraph describing the best way to present the material in a clear and interesting manner.

_____

_____

_____

_____

_____

Conventions

Use Articles as Adjectives

DIRECTIONS Write two sentences that use one or more of the following articles: *a, an,* and *the.* Circle the articles in your sentences.

_____

_____

_____

_____

Students write routinely for a range of tasks, purposes, and audiences. Students practice various conventions of standard English.

Name _____

DIRECTIONS Write a sentence using each word.

survive   desert   lizards

_____

_____

_____

Write in Response to Reading

Look at the photograph of Antarctica on p. 12. How does the image help you understand the characteristics of dry places?

_____

_____

_____

_____

Students demonstrate contextual understanding of Benchmark Vocabulary. Students read text closely and use text evidence in their written answers.

Name _____

Plan and Prewrite Decide on a topic for an informational article. Gather information by talking to people, making observations, and reading about the topic. Take notes below or on a separate sheet of paper.

_____

_____

_____

_____

_____

Conventions

Form and Use Adjectives

DIRECTIONS Complete each sentence with the correct form of the adjective.

1. Jessie is the _____ (*tall,* superlative) girl in her family.

2. New Mexico is _____ (*warm,* comparative) than Massachusetts during the winter.

3. The _____ (*old,* superlative) person in the world is 117 years old.

Students write routinely for a range of tasks, purposes, and audiences. Students practice various conventions of standard English.

Name _____

DIRECTIONS Write a sentence using each word.

    sand grains   dunes   atmosphere   rainbow   scattered

_____

_____

_____

_____

_____

_____

_____

Write in Response to Reading

Reread p. 16. How is sand formed? How do the photograph and caption at the bottom of the page help you understand that process?

_____

_____

_____

_____

_____

_____

Students demonstrate contextual understanding of Benchmark Vocabulary. Students read text closely and use text evidence in their written answers.

Name _____

Backyard Safari

Because I live in the city, I rarely see animals that I read about in school. When Dad takes me to the park, I see pigeons and squirrels. Boring! I want to see snakes and rabbits.

Last weekend I stayed with Aunt Marie in the country. Instead of going to the park, I played in Aunt Marie's backyard.

When we arrived at Aunt Marie's, I found her fixing breakfast and wearing a strange hat. "What's that on your head?" I asked.

"It's my safari hat!" She held up a smaller one and tossed it to me. Aunt Marie explained that we were going on a backyard safari.

I inhaled my breakfast. Then we set out toward the yard with binoculars and a magnifying glass.

"Do you hear that?" Aunt Marie asked.

I heard what sounded like a tiny jackhammer. She handed me the binoculars and told me to look high up in the tree. I soon found the source of the noise. It was a woodpecker with a red head.

Aunt Marie said that rabbits love to rest under her rose bushes. We lay in the grass and waited. As we waited, she told me all about the critters that call her backyard home—opossum, raccoons, chipmunks, and snakes. Some like to come out early in the morning, others at night.

Then something caught my eye. It was a ball of fur with a nose that was wiggling. "A rabbit," I whispered, even though I wanted to yell. Who knew I could see so much wildlife on a backyard safari!

Students read text closely to determine what the text says.

Name _____

Gather Evidence Circle two details in the text that show the narrator was excited about the backyard safari.

Gather Evidence: Extend Your Ideas Work with a partner, and discuss how changing just one of these details would affect the story.

Ask Questions Write two questions you would ask an expert about animals that live near humans. Underline any words in the text that could help answer the first question. Underline twice any words in the text that could help answer the second question.

_____

_____

Ask Questions: Extend Your Ideas Did you underline any words in the text that would answer your questions? If the answer is yes, explain. If the answer is no, write an additional question that is answered in the text, and include that answer with your new question on the lines below.

_____

_____

Make Your Case Circle words in the story that show how the narrator's home and Aunt Marie's home are alike and different.

Make Your Case: Extend Your Ideas Write a sentence or two explaining why the differences between their homes are important in the story.

_____

_____

Students read text closely to determine what the text says.

Name _____

Draft On a separate sheet of paper, draft an article using the information you gathered in Lesson 12. Begin with an introductory paragraph about your topic. Then develop your topic in body paragraphs with facts, definitions, and details. Finally, write an interesting conclusion to your article.

Conventions

Produce Sentences Using Adjectives

DIRECTIONS Write three sentences that include at least one adjective. Circle the adjective(s) in each sentence.

_____

_____

_____

Students write routinely for a range of tasks, purposes, and audiences. Students practice various conventions of standard English.

Name _____

DIRECTIONS Write a sentence using each word.

thunderstorm   lightning   electricity

_____

_____

_____

_____

Write in Response to Reading

Reread pp. 22–23. Why do you think thunderstorms happen more frequently during the spring and summer?

_____

_____

_____

_____

_____

_____

Students demonstrate contextual understanding of Benchmark Vocabulary. Students read text closely and use text evidence in their written answers.

Name _____

Explain Scientific Ideas and Concepts

DIRECTIONS Using evidence from the text, answer the following questions about pp. 22–25 from *About Earth*.

1. What always occurs along with thunder during a storm?

   _____

   _____

2. What causes lightning?

   _____

   _____

3. What contributes to the formation of both wind and thunderstorms?

   _____

   _____

4. Where do the coolest winds begin?

   _____

   _____

Students analyze and respond to literary and informational text.

Name _____

Revise On a separate sheet of paper, revise the article you drafted in Lesson 13. Make sure your topic is clear and your article includes facts and details that support your main idea.

Coordinating Conjunctions

DIRECTIONS Underline the coordinating conjunction in each sentence, and identify whether it connects two words, two phrases, or two sentences.

1. Lois will not go with us to the play, but she will join us for dinner.

_____

2. Frances told Juan he could have candy or soda as a treat.

_____

3. I always avoid going to the grocery store and driving on the highway during the holidays.

_____

Students write routinely for a range of tasks, purposes, and audiences. Students practice various conventions of standard English.

Benchmark Vocabulary

Name _____

DIRECTIONS Write a sentence using each word.

earthquake   volcano   oozing   plates   magma

_____

_____

_____

_____

_____

_____

_____

Write in Response to Reading

How are earthquakes and volcanoes similar? How are earthquakes and volcanoes different?

_____

_____

_____

_____

_____

Students demonstrate contextual understanding of Benchmark Vocabulary. Students read text closely and use text evidence in their written answers.

Name _____

Edit and Present On a separate sheet of paper, edit your article. Check the spelling, capitalization, punctuation, and grammar.

Coordinating Conjunctions

DIRECTIONS Circle the coordinating conjunction in each sentence. Identify whether the conjunction creates a compound subject, verb, or direct object.

1. Volcanoes erupt and spew magma. _____

2. You can take a toy and a book with you. _____

3. Lyle or Fran will pick him up from the airport. _____

Students write routinely for a range of tasks, purposes, and audiences. Students practice various conventions of standard English.

Name _____

Final Syllable *-le*

DIRECTIONS On the lines, write the two syllables that make up each word.

1. _____ + _____ = giggle

2. _____ + _____ = riddle

3. _____ + _____ = cycle

4. _____ + _____ = wheedle

5. _____ + _____ = warble

6. _____ + _____ = table

7. _____ + _____ = mumble

8. _____ + _____ = saddle

9. _____ + _____ = tingle

10. _____ + _____ = turtle

DIRECTIONS Use words from the Word Bank to complete the sentences. You will not use all of the words.

Word Bank

noodle	poodle	people	uncle	juggle	trouble

11. My _____ was waving his arms around.

12. He was trying to _____ the spaghetti on his fork.

13. Every time he got a _____, he lost it again.

14. That's because our big, smart _____ grabbed it!

15. Who knew eating pasta could be such _____?

Students apply grade-level phonics and word analysis skills.

Name _____

DIRECTIONS Write a sentence using each word.

contain   liquid   oozing   survive

_____

_____

_____

_____

_____

_____

Write in Response to Reading

How do the definitions in the glossary on p. 32 help you better understand ideas in the text? Use specific examples from the text in your answer.

_____

_____

_____

_____

_____

_____

Students demonstrate contextual understanding of Benchmark Vocabulary. Students read text closely and use text evidence in their written answers.

Name _____

Publish and Present Write down notes and ideas for presenting your article to the class. Practice presenting your article as though you are a reporter delivering a news story, including illustrations and other text features. Then present your article to the class.

_____

_____

_____

_____

_____

Coordinating Conjunctions

DIRECTIONS Circle the coordinating conjunction in each sentence, and underline the two phrases that it connects.

1. Christine always arrives on time but never buys her ticket in advance.

2. Keep your phone in your pocket or in your bag.

3. Emma likes reading books and listening to music.

Students write routinely for a range of tasks, purposes, and audiences. Students practice various conventions of standard English.

Name _____

DIRECTIONS Write a sentence using each word.

phases   fascinated   planet

_____

_____

_____

_____

Write in Response to Reading

Review the text features the authors use in *The Moon Seems to Change,*
Treasure in the Trees, and *About Earth.* Identify the most useful text
feature in each text, and explain how it helped you understand a key idea
or message.

_____

_____

_____

_____

_____

Students demonstrate contextual
understanding of Benchmark Vocabulary.
Students read text closely and use text
evidence in their written answers.

Name _____

Text Features

DIRECTIONS Using evidence from the texts, answer the following questions about *The Moon Seems to Change, Treasure in the Trees,* and *About Earth.*

1. Look at the illustration on p. 3 of *About Earth.* Now look at the top illustration on p. 45 of *The Moon Seems to Change.* Both show Earth and the sun. How are these illustrations different? Why are they different?

   _____

   _____

   _____

   _____

   _____

2. How do the headings in *About Earth* and *Treasure in the Trees* help you understand the texts?

   _____

   _____

   _____

   _____

   _____

3. Which text feature can you find in all three texts?

   _____

   _____

Students analyze and respond to literary and informational text.

Name _____

Take Notes and Sort Evidence Choose a topic and research it. Gather evidence from that research, and in the space below or on a separate sheet of paper, sort the evidence into categories. Use a graphic organizer to help you sort the evidence, if necessary.

_____

_____

_____

_____

_____

Conventions

Use Coordinating Conjunctions

DIRECTIONS Complete each sentence with the correct coordinating conjunction.

1. Fred is friendly _____ funny, so everyone likes him.

2. The bus is either early _____ late, but it's never on time.

3. We can study for the test here _____ at the library, but we have to make a decision soon.

Students write routinely for a range of tasks, purposes, and audiences. Students practice various conventions of standard English.

Name _____

DIRECTIONS Write a sentence using the word.

observation

_____

_____

_____

_____

Write in Response to Reading

Identify one detail from *The Moon Seems to Change, Treasure in the Trees,* and *About Earth* that was key in helping you understand a main idea or central message in the text. Explain how it helped you understand that idea or message.

_____

_____

_____

_____

_____

_____

Students demonstrate contextual understanding of Benchmark Vocabulary. Students read text closely and use text evidence in their written answers.

Name _____

Gather Information to Build Knowledge Observe something in nature, using the texts you have read as models. On another sheet of paper, record your observations by making sketches and by writing and answering two or three questions that make your observations more accurate and detailed.

Use Coordinating Conjunctions

DIRECTIONS Write three compound sentences that include coordinating conjunctions.

_____

_____

_____

_____

_____

_____

Students write routinely for a range of tasks, purposes, and audiences. Students practice various conventions of standard English.

Name _____

Compound Words

DIRECTIONS Identify the two words that make up each compound word. Write the words.

1. _____ + _____ = sunglasses

2. _____ + _____ = railroad

3. _____ + _____ = haircut

4. _____ + _____ = firehouse

5. _____ + _____ = popcorn

6. _____ + _____ = myself

7. _____ + _____ = greenhouse

8. _____ + _____ = backyard

9. _____ + _____ = rainwater

10. _____ + _____ = sunflower

DIRECTIONS Choose the compound word to complete each sentence. Write the word on the line. Draw a line between the two words that make up each compound word.

_____ **11.** My (grandfather/uncle) lives on a farm.

_____ **12.** I help him (whenever/when) I visit.

_____ **13.** Last winter, there was a terrible (blizzard/snowstorm).

_____ **14.** We had to work (quickly/outside) in the cold.

_____ **15.** It's (sometimes/often) difficult to be a farmer.

Students apply grade-level phonics and word analysis skills.

Name _____

DIRECTIONS Write a sentence using each word.

pioneers   migrated   preserve   plentiful   scarce

_____

_____

_____

_____

_____

_____

Write in Response to Reading

Read the final paragraph on page 76. Do you think the Athabascans succeeded at "learning the new ways of a new world," while still practicing the old ways? Use details from the text to support your opinion.

_____

_____

_____

_____

_____

Students demonstrate contextual understanding of Benchmark Vocabulary. Students read text closely and use text evidence in their written answers.

Name _____

Research and Gather Information Use "Finding Food" and "Camping" in the text and your own knowledge to come up with details that could be used in a story. First, record details about old and new ways of finding food and setting up camp using the text and your own knowledge. Then, write a few sentences to explain how these details could be used in a story.

_____

_____

_____

_____

_____

Conventions

Start Sentences with Capital Letters

DIRECTIONS Rewrite the sentences below and capitalize the appropriate words.

we all had to chip in to buy the toy boat. it was very expensive, so we saved our money for three months. after we had saved enough money, we went to the store and bought it.

_____

_____

_____

_____

Students write routinely for a range of tasks, purposes, and audiences. Students practice various conventions of standard English.

Name _____

DIRECTIONS Write a sentence using each word.

pioneers   migrated   scarce

_____

_____

_____

_____

Write in Response to Reading

Read page 65 and explain why the Athabascans chose to live like their ancestors did. Be sure to use evidence from the text.

_____

_____

_____

_____

_____

Students demonstrate contextual understanding of Benchmark Vocabulary. Students read text closely and use text evidence in their written answers.

Name _____

Words Used for Effect

DIRECTIONS Using evidence from the text, answer the following questions about *The Athabascans: Old Ways and New Ways*.

1. Read the second paragraph on page 65. Find the word *pioneer*. Why did the author choose the word *pioneer?*

   _____

   _____

   _____

2. Revisit the section "Camping." Read the sentence "We all had to chip in to make sure everyone was fed." What does "chip in" mean? Which details from the text help readers understand its meaning?

   _____

   _____

3. In the first paragraph in the section "One-Room Schoolhouses," read the sentence that begins, "He would have to watch out . . ." What effect do the words *big* and *hungry* have on the reader? What is the author's purpose for including them?

   _____

   _____

   _____

4. In the section "One-Room Schoolhouses," read the sentence beginning, "Green, fiery, wolf orbs . . ." What effect do these words have on the reader?

   _____

   _____

Students analyze and respond to literary and informational text.

Name _____

Write Notes for a Story Read "Getting Around" and "One-Room Schoolhouses" in the text, and take notes on details that interest you. Write a few sentences that explain how these details could be used in a story, as well as story ideas you came up with as you took notes.

_____

_____

_____

_____

_____

_____

Conventions

Capitalize Appropriate Words in Titles

DIRECTIONS Rewrite each title and capitalize the appropriate words.

1. city homes _____

2. the year of miss agnes _____

3. the song of sky and sand _____

Students write routinely for a range of tasks, purposes, and audiences. Students practice various conventions of standard English.

Name _____

DIRECTIONS Write a sentence using the word.

mileage

_____

_____

_____

Write in Response to Reading

Read the dialogue about speaking English on pages 9–10. Based on
the conversation about English, do you think the new teacher is a good
teacher? Why or why not? Support your opinion with text evidence.

_____

_____

_____

_____

_____

Students demonstrate contextual
understanding of Benchmark Vocabulary.
Students read text closely and use text
evidence in their written answers.

Name _____

A Visit to Vietnam

Benjamin's family left Vietnam when he was just a baby. Benjamin's dad had gotten a better job in Seattle, Washington. Every couple of years, his family went back to Vietnam to visit. This summer they were going for their longest visit yet—all summer!

After a long flight, their plane finally landed in Ho Chi Minh City. Benjamin couldn't wait to get to his grandparents' house. After his family picked up their luggage, they took a taxi through the busy streets. Benjamin had forgotten how many motorcycles and scooters zipped around the city.

The cab drove them past markets and street vendors. Benjamin licked his lips. He loved the fresh fruit and other delicious food in Vietnam.

Benjamin also loved looking at the different kinds of buildings. In one block, there were buildings that were hundreds of years old. Then, just a few blocks away, there were new shopping centers. Some of the stores and restaurants were the same ones Benjamin's family went to in Seattle.

Benjamin couldn't wait to see his grandparents. He loved pho, the special noodle soup his grandmother made. He liked sitting in the shady courtyard with his grandfather, who told stories about growing up in Vietnam.

His grandparents had also promised to take him to the beach this summer. Benjamin couldn't wait to go swimming in the South China Sea! There was so much he wanted to see and do. This was going to be the best summer ever!

Students read text closely to determine what the text says.

Name _____

Gather Evidence How does Benjamin feel about his trip to Vietnam?
Circle 5 words and phrases from the story that support your answer.

_____

_____

_____

Ask Questions Write 2–3 questions you have about Vietnam that can be answered from the text.

_____

_____

_____

Make Your Case What do you think is the main idea that the writer wants to share? Underline 2–3 key details that support the main idea.

_____

_____

_____

Students read text closely to determine what the text says.

Name _____

Genre Describe a story you would like to write. Then explain what genre it would be and why.

_____

_____

_____

_____

_____

_____

Conventions

Capitalize Proper Nouns

DIRECTIONS Rewrite each sentence and capitalize the proper nouns.

1. Her sister laura goes to washington high school. _____

_____

2. I visited aunt meg in dallas last november. _____

_____

3. Maria is from spain, but she lives in brazil now. _____

_____

Students write routinely for a range of tasks, purposes, and audiences. Students practice various conventions of standard English.

Name _____

DIRECTIONS Write a sentence using the word.

nuisance

_____

_____

_____

_____

Write in Response to Reading

Read the description of making clothes on pages 20–24. Write a paragraph that explains the process of making mittens, boots, or snowshoes. Write each step in the sequence, including the tasks done by Grandpa, Mamma, Grandma, and the sisters, Fred and Bokko. Support your explanation with evidence from the text.

_____

_____

_____

_____

_____

_____

Students demonstrate contextual
understanding of Benchmark Vocabulary.
Students read text closely and use text
evidence in their written answers.

Name _____

Character

DIRECTIONS Using evidence from the text, answer the following questions about pages 14–15 of *The Year of Miss Agnes*.

1. How does Mamma feel about Fred going to school? What evidence from the text supports your answer?

_____

_____

_____

2. How does Fred feel about going to school? What evidence from the text supports your answer?

_____

_____

_____

_____

_____

3. How does Bokko feel about Fred going to school? What evidence from the text supports your answer?

_____

_____

4. What is Fred able to do that Mamma cannot do? What does this reveal about her character?

_____

_____

Students analyze and respond to literary and informational text.

Name _____

Establish a Situation Write an opening paragraph that introduces the main character, describes the setting, and establishes the situation for your story.

_____

_____

_____

_____

_____

Conventions

Use Adverbs

DIRECTIONS Complete each sentence with an adverb.

1. Nora walked _____ to her seat.

2. Marion read the book _____.

3. Jesse is _____ sick.

Students write routinely for a range of tasks, purposes, and audiences. Students practice various conventions of standard English.

Benchmark Vocabulary

Name _____

DIRECTIONS Write a sentence using each word.

cache   margin   freight

_____

_____

_____

_____

Write in Response to Reading

Read the last two paragraphs on pages 37–38. Was it a good idea for Miss Agnes to be "so picky" about her students' writing? Support your opinion with evidence from the text.

_____

_____

_____

_____

_____

Students demonstrate contextual understanding of Benchmark Vocabulary. Students read text closely and use text evidence in their written answers.

Name _____

Introduce a Narrator and Characters Write a character sketch for a character that would appear in your narrative. Describe the character's physical traits, actions, motivations, and feelings.

_____

_____

_____

_____

_____

Function of Adverbs in a Sentence

DIRECTIONS Write a sentence with an adverb that performs the function identified, and underline the adverb.

1. Shows Location: _____

2. Shows Time: _____

3. Shows Frequency: _____

Students write routinely for a range of tasks, purposes, and audiences. Students practice various conventions of standard English.

Name _____

Consonant Blends (2- and 3-Letter)

DIRECTIONS Read the story. Underline the words with **2-letter consonant blends** (for example, *fl, pr,* and *st*). Then write the underlined words on the lines.

Ella stuffed her feet into her boots and trudged outdoors. As she drew close to the school, she saw her friends filling balloons. They filled them so full that they broke! Then one balloon flew up into the sky. Ella laughed. The girls began releasing full balloons, laughing as they watched them fly toward the clouds.

1. _____
2. _____
3. _____
4. _____
5. _____

6. _____
7. _____
8. _____
9. _____
10. _____

DIRECTIONS Read each word out loud and listen for a **3-letter blend,** such as *squ, spl, thr,* or *str.* Then write two more words that start with the same blend. Underline the three-letter blend in each word you write.

11. straw _____

12. splurge _____

13. squeak _____

14. thread _____

15. strike _____

Students apply grade-level phonics and word analysis skills.

Name _____

DIRECTIONS Write a sentence using each word.

continents   trader

_____

_____

_____

_____

Write in Response to Reading

Read the final paragraph of page 46. Write a paragraph explaining why the children would not get tired of having Miss Agnes for a teacher. Support your answer with text evidence.

_____

_____

_____

_____

_____

Students demonstrate contextual understanding of Benchmark Vocabulary. Students read text closely and use text evidence in their written answers.

Name _____

Organize an Event Sequence Write a paragraph that describes an event sequence in which one event affects or causes another. Organize the events so that they unfold naturally.

_____

_____

_____

_____

_____

_____

Form Superlative Adverbs

DIRECTIONS Complete each sentence with a superlative adverb.

1. Myra ate her dinner _____.

2. Lou Ann works _____ early in the morning.

3. My dog Charlie runs the _____.

Students write routinely for a range of tasks, purposes, and audiences. Students practice various conventions of standard English.

Name _____

DIRECTIONS Write a sentence using the word.

deaf

_____

_____

_____

_____

Write in Response to Reading

Read the first full paragraph on page 53, which begins, "When Mamma stamped . . ." Write an opinion on whether Grandpa should have defended Mamma when she stomped out the door. Support your opinion with text evidence.

_____

_____

_____

_____

_____

Students demonstrate contextual
understanding of Benchmark Vocabulary.
Students read text closely and use text
evidence in their written answers.

Name _____

Character

DIRECTIONS Using evidence from the text, answer the following questions about Chapter 8 from *The Year of Miss Agnes.*

1. What does Bokko's trip to the school to bring Fred her lunch reveal about Bokko's character?

   _____

   _____

2. How does Bokko's trip to the school to bring Fred's lunch affect Miss Agnes's actions?

   _____

   _____

3. What does Miss Agnes's conversation with Mamma reveal about Miss Agnes's character?

   _____

   _____

4. What conflict does the conversation between Mamma and Miss Agnes lead to? Explain how the two events are related.

   _____

   _____

5. What does this event reveal about Mamma's character?

   _____

   _____

Students analyze and respond to literary and informational text.

Name _____

Use Temporal Words and Phrases to Signal Event Order Write a paragraph that uses temporal words and phrases to signal the order of events in an event sequence. Use the event sequence from Lesson 6 or create a new event sequence.

_____

_____

_____

_____

_____

_____

Conventions

Use Adverbs in a Sentence

DIRECTIONS Write a sentence with each adverb below.

1. slowly _____

2. very _____

3. too _____

Students write routinely for a range of tasks, purposes, and audiences. Students practice various conventions of standard English.

Benchmark Vocabulary

Name _____

DIRECTIONS Write a sentence using the word.

catalog

_____

_____

_____

_____

Write in Response to Reading

Read page 67. Write a paragraph about what you think would be a better way to ask someone to dance. Support your opinion with text evidence.

_____

_____

_____

_____

_____

Students demonstrate contextual understanding of Benchmark Vocabulary. Students read text closely and use text evidence in their written answers.

Name _____

Use Dialogue to Develop Experiences Write a skit that tells more about an event that was mentioned only briefly in *The Year of Miss Agnes*. Use dialogue to develop the characters' experiences.

_____

_____

_____

_____

_____

_____

Conventions

Review Commas in Dialogue

DIRECTIONS Write three sentences of dialogue. Place commas in the appropriate places.

_____

_____

_____

_____

_____

Students write routinely for a range of tasks, purposes, and audiences. Students practice various conventions of standard English.

Name _____

DIRECTIONS Write a sentence using each word.

snares   goggled   bluff

_____

_____

_____

_____

Write in Response to Reading

Read page 76, starting with the paragraph that begins, "Miss Agnes told him . . ." Was Miss Agnes right to appear angry with the students? State your opinion and support it with text evidence.

_____

_____

_____

_____

_____

Students demonstrate contextual understanding of Benchmark Vocabulary. Students read text closely and use text evidence in their written answers.

Name _____

Use Dialogue to Show Character Responses Write dialogue that shows characters' responses. Use the characters you created in previous lessons or think of new characters.

_____

_____

_____

_____

_____

Review Quotation Marks in Dialogue

DIRECTIONS Write three sentences of dialogue using quotation marks correctly.

_____

_____

_____

_____

_____

Students write routinely for a range of tasks, purposes, and audiences. Students practice various conventions of standard English.

Name _____

DIRECTIONS Write a sentence using each word.

brittle   wringer

_____

_____

_____

_____

Write in Response to Reading

Read pages 94–95. Choose one student in the story, and tell what
Miss Agnes said that he or she was good at doing. Then tell how she knew
what the student's talent was. Use text evidence to support your answer.

_____

_____

_____

_____

_____

_____

Students demonstrate contextual
understanding of Benchmark Vocabulary.
Students read text closely and use text
evidence in their written answers.

Name _____

Character

DIRECTIONS Using evidence from the text, answer the following questions about pages 92–95 from *The Year of Miss Agnes.*

1. How do the books Miss Agnes writes for each student encourage the students to read in two ways?

_____

_____

_____

2. What else does Miss Agnes do to help the students improve their reading skills?

_____

_____

_____

3. What does the assignment from Miss Agnes help reveal about Fred's character?

_____

_____

4. Why do you think Miss Agnes tells each student what he or she is good at?

_____

_____

_____

_____

Students analyze and respond to literary and informational text.

Name _____

Use Descriptions to Develop Experiences Create a character sketch of
Miss Agnes that describes her and the impact she has on the community.

_____

_____

_____

_____

_____

_____

Conventions

Use an Exclamation Mark in Dialogue

DIRECTIONS Write a dialogue below. Use at least two exclamation
marks to show characters' strong feelings.

_____

_____

_____

_____

_____

_____

Students write routinely for a range of
tasks, purposes, and audiences. Students
practice various conventions of standard
English.

Name _____

Consonant Digraphs

DIRECTIONS Write **sh, th, ph, ch, tch,** or **ng** to complete each word. Write the whole word on the line to the left.

_____ **1.** Maria's family pur____ased a house.

_____ **2.** Her mo____er decided to paint it.

_____ **3.** She bought bru____es and buckets.

_____ **4.** Back home, she put on old clo____es.

_____ **5.** Then she pa____ ed nail holes in the walls.

_____ **6.** Maria was goi____ to help choose colors.

_____ **7.** She ____oned a friend to talk it over.

_____ **8.** The two of them made some ____oices.

_____ **9.** Maria wanted ____ades of blue.

_____ **10.** Her brother ____ose red instead.

DIRECTIONS Read each definition. Then write **sh, th, wh, ph,** or **ng** to complete the word that matches.

11. An award that looks like a statue or cup   tro_____y

12. A mammal that lives in the ocean   _____ale

13. Playground equipment that gets pushed   swi_____

14. A person who participates in sports   a_____lete

15. Something a person can shrug   _____oulder

Students apply grade-level phonics and word analysis skills.

Name _____

DIRECTIONS Write a sentence using the word.

bunks

_____

_____

_____

_____

Write in Response to Reading

Read page 102. Do you think "young brains" are better than "old brains"?
Use text evidence to support your opinion.

_____

_____

_____

_____

_____

Students demonstrate contextual
understanding of Benchmark Vocabulary.
Students read text closely and use text
evidence in their written answers.

Name _____

Use Descriptions to Show Responses Look at the dialogue you wrote in Lesson 9. Write a paragraph that uses descriptions instead of dialogue to show a character's response.

_____

_____

_____

_____

_____

_____

Conventions

Use a Question Mark in Dialogue

DIRECTIONS Read page 105 in *The Year of Miss Agnes*. Write two questions that students might ask Miss Agnes. Place a question mark in the appropriate place in each line of dialogue.

_____

_____

_____

_____

Students write routinely for range of tasks, purposes, and audiences. Students practice various conventions of standard English.

Name _____

DIRECTIONS Write a sentence using the word.

invented

_____

_____

_____

_____

Write in Response to Reading

Read the first complete paragraph on page 111. Explain why so many things reminded Fred and Bokko of Miss Agnes. Use text evidence to support your answer.

_____

_____

_____

_____

_____

Students demonstrate contextual understanding of Benchmark Vocabulary. Students read text closely and use text evidence in their written answers.

Name _____

Character

DIRECTIONS Using evidence from the text, answer the following questions about pages 109–111 from *The Year of Miss Agnes*.

1. How have Bokko's feelings changed about being around other people?

   _____

   _____

2. How do Bokko's actions around her family change as a result?

   _____

   _____

3. What are Fred and Bokko able to do during fish camp because they have been in school?

   _____

   _____

4. How does Mamma respond to Fred and Bokko using the skills they learned in school? How does Fred describe Mamma's feelings?

   _____

   _____

   _____

5. Why do you think Mamma's actions do not show her feelings?

   _____

   _____

   _____

Students analyze and respond to literary and informational text.

Name _____

Provide a Sense of Closure Write an ending for your story that provides a sense of closure.

_____

_____

_____

_____

_____

Review Subject-Verb Agreement in Sentences

DIRECTIONS Write three sentences with correct subject-verb agreement. Include at least one sentence with a singular subject and one sentence with a plural subject.

_____

_____

_____

_____

Students write routinely for a range of tasks, purposes, and audiences. Students practice various conventions of standard English.

Name _____

DIRECTIONS Write a sentence using each word.

migrated   plentiful   cache   margin   brittle

_____

_____

_____

_____

_____

_____

Write in Response to Reading

How do *The Athabascans: Old Ways and New Ways* and *The Year of Miss Agnes* help you understand how people can learn to practice both old and new ways? Use text evidence to support your answer.

_____

_____

_____

_____

_____

Students demonstrate contextual
understanding of Benchmark Vocabulary.
Students read text closely and use text
evidence in their written answers.

A Day at School in Japan

Have you ever wondered how a school day in Japan might compare to one of yours?

Like many students in the United States, many Japanese elementary school students start their day around 8:30 a.m. and end around 3:00 p.m. They have math and reading classes. They listen to announcements at the start of the day. The teacher takes attendance. During the week, students might gather for an assembly where the principal or someone else talks to them.

There are a number of differences too. For example, in the United States, students learn handwriting. In Japan, students learn *shodo,* or calligraphy. This involves dipping a brush into ink and writing symbols. The symbols stand for words. Students in Japan also have a class where they learn how to cook and sew.

If you think school is hard in America, think about what students in Japan must do. They often have more homework than students in the United States do. They also spend at least six more weeks in school each year. Some schools also assign chores to students. Sweeping and cleaning the floor, wiping the board, and emptying the trash are some of these chores.

If you were an American student in a Japanese school, do you think it would be difficult to adjust to these differences? Remember, you would have to do everything in a completely different language, too.

Students read text closely to determine what the text says.

Name _____

Gather Evidence How does a day at school in Japan compare to your school day in the United States?

_____

_____

_____

Ask Questions Write three questions you would ask a student from Japan about his or her day at school. Underline sentences or phrases from the text that answer your questions.

_____

_____

_____

Make Your Case What is the most interesting detail you can learn from the images that support the idea that schools in Japan are different from schools here? Can you find that detail in the text?

_____

_____

_____

Students read text closely to determine what the text says.

Name _____

Review the Elements of Narrative Writing Write a paragraph for a narrative, using one or more of the elements of narrative writing.

_____

_____

_____

_____

_____

Subject-Verb Agreement with Regular Verbs

DIRECTIONS Complete each sentence with the correct form of the verb in parentheses.

1. Laura and Felicia _____ (climb) the hill yesterday.

2. Sylvia _____ (march) up the stairs to her room and starts her homework.

3. Wendy _____ (talk) to her best friend as they walk to class.

Students write routinely for a range of tasks, purposes, and audiences. Students practice various conventions of standard English.

Name _____

DIRECTIONS Write a sentence using each word.

suitor	threshold	mourned	consent	summons
morsel	feast	unnatural	exchange	

_____

_____

_____

_____

_____

_____

_____

Write in Response to Reading

Read page 86 of *The Frog Princess*. Write a few sentences explaining how the girl felt when she was with the Frog People. How do her feelings about the Frog People shape the rest of the story? Support your answer with text evidence.

_____

_____

_____

_____

_____

Students demonstrate contextual
understanding of Benchmark Vocabulary.
Students read text closely and use text
evidence in their written answers.

Name _____

Plan and Prewrite a Narrative Gather information and take notes below on characters and events in legends to plan an extension of *The Frog Princess*. Then use the Story Sequence B graphic organizer to plan your narrative.

_____

_____

_____

_____

_____

_____

Conventions

Subject-Verb Agreement with Irregular Verbs in Sentences

DIRECTIONS Use each irregular verb below in a sentence with the tense and subject identified.

1. *take* (present tense, singular subject) _____

_____

2. *do* (past tense, plural subject) _____

_____

3. *go* (past tense, singular subject) _____

_____

Students write routinely for a range of tasks, purposes, and audiences. Students practice various conventions of standard English.

Name _____

DIRECTIONS Write a sentence using each word.

consent   exchange   summons

_____

_____

_____

_____

Write in Response to Reading

Does the girl's attitude in *The Frog Princess* change as the story goes along? Support your opinion using text evidence.

_____

_____

_____

_____

_____

Students demonstrate contextual understanding of Benchmark Vocabulary. Students read text closely and use text evidence in their written answers.

Determine the Central Message

DIRECTIONS Using evidence from the text, answer the following questions about *The Frog Princess*.

1. What key details from the story show the reader how the Frog Princess feels about being with the Frog People?

_____

_____

_____

_____

2. What key details from the story show the reader how the Frog Princess feels about being at home again?

_____

_____

_____

3. What key details from the story show the reader how the Frog Princess feels about returning to live with the Frog People?

_____

_____

_____

_____

4. What central message do these details help communicate?

_____

_____

Students analyze and respond to literary and informational text.

Name _____

Draft a Narrative Draft your extension of *The Frog Princess.* Be sure to establish a situation with a problem or conflict, include a short, organized sequence of events, and resolve the situation.

_____

_____

_____

_____

_____

_____

Conventions

Review Simple Sentences

DIRECTIONS Write three simple sentences. One sentence should have a plural subject.

_____

_____

_____

_____

_____

_____

Students write routinely for a range of tasks, purposes, and audiences. Students practice various conventions of standard English.

Name _____

Contractions

DIRECTIONS Use each pair of words to form a contraction. Write the contraction on the line.

_____ **1.** have not   _____ **8.** I would

_____ **2.** when is   _____ **9.** let us

_____ **3.** did not   _____ **10.** they are

_____ **4.** they will   _____ **11.** that is

_____ **5.** she is   _____ **12.** he would

_____ **6.** you will   _____ **13.** was not

_____ **7.** we would   _____ **14.** you had

DIRECTIONS Use the words in parentheses to make a contraction and complete each sentence. Write the contraction on the line.

_____ **15.** Javier (has not) planted a garden before.

_____ **16.** This year he has decided (he would) like to try.

_____ **17.** His dad says (they will) work on it together.

_____ **18.** Javier's sister told them it (was not) warm enough to begin.

_____ **19.** She said seeds won't grow when (it is) too cold.

_____ **20.** Javier said, "Gosh! (I have) never heard that before!"

Students apply grade-level phonics and word analysis skills.

Name _____

DIRECTIONS Write a sentence using each word.

threshold   morsel   unnatural

_____

_____

_____

_____

Write in Response to Reading

Read pages 99–100 of *The Frog Princess*. Think about the actions of the girl, her family, and the shaman. Then write a few sentences describing the events on those pages. Be sure to describe the events in the same order that they happen in the text, and use text evidence in your description.

_____

_____

_____

_____

_____

Students demonstrate contextual understanding of Benchmark Vocabulary. Students read text closely and use text evidence in their written answers.

Name _____

Revise a Narrative Revise your story. Emphasize the traits of your characters, and make sure that your event sequence flows naturally and ends with a logical resolution to the problem in the story.

_____

_____

_____

_____

_____

Conventions

Define Compound Sentences

DIRECTIONS Underline the two independent clauses in each compound sentence, and circle the coordinating conjunction that connects them.

1. The woman spoke calmly to her grandchildren, but they did not pay attention to her.

2. My brother can go to Anderson Middle School, or he can be homeschooled.

3. Nina went to the park, and she played baseball with her friends.

Students write routinely for a range of tasks, purposes, and audiences. Students practice various conventions of standard English.

Name _____

DIRECTIONS Write a sentence using each word.

freight   continents   mourned   feast

_____

_____

_____

_____

_____

Write in Response to Reading

The parents in both texts make decisions about their children's lives based on their own experiences. Should parents make these decisions for their children? Why or why not? Support your opinion with text evidence.

_____

_____

_____

_____

_____

Students demonstrate contextual understanding of Benchmark Vocabulary. Students read text closely and use text evidence in their written answers.

Name _____

Compare and Contrast

DIRECTIONS Using evidence from the texts, answer the following questions about *The Year of Miss Agnes* and *The Frog Princess*.

1. What is one way that the author develops the central message that people should accept new possibilities without ignoring old traditions in *The Year of Miss Agnes*?

   _____

   _____

   _____

2. Is this idea developed in *The Frog Princess*? If so, what key details help develop this message?

   _____

   _____

   _____

3. What is one way that the author develops the central message that people should respect others' choices in *The Frog Princess*?

   _____

   _____

4. Is this idea developed in *The Year of Miss Agnes*? If so, what key details help develop this message?

   _____

   _____

   _____

Students analyze and respond to literary and informational text.

Name _____

Edit a Narrative Correct any errors in grammar, spelling, punctuation, and capitalization in your story. Then, using those corrections and feedback from a partner, write your final draft on a separate sheet of paper.

Conventions

Produce Compound Sentences

DIRECTIONS Combine each pair of sentences using either a coordinating conjunction or a semicolon.

1. Norman wanted to buy the guitar. It was too expensive.

_____

_____

2. He did have enough money for a small drum. He bought one.

_____

_____

3. He liked playing the drum. It helped him express his emotions.

_____

_____

Students write routinely for a range of tasks, purposes, and audiences. Students practice various conventions of standard English.

Name _____

DIRECTIONS Write a sentence using each word.

pioneers   preserve   scarce   nuisance   snares   goggled

_____

_____

_____

_____

_____

_____

_____

Write in Response to Reading

Think about what the three texts tell you about the differences between old ways and new ways. Why do people want to live in old ways? Why do they want to try new ways? Support your opinion with text evidence.

_____

_____

_____

_____

_____

Students demonstrate contextual understanding of Benchmark Vocabulary. Students read text closely and use text evidence in their written answers.

Name _____

Publish and Present Present your work by acting out scenes from the story you wrote. Write the scenes you will act out below or on a separate sheet of paper.

_____

_____

_____

_____

_____

Produce Compound Sentences

DIRECTIONS Write a compound sentence with each coordinating conjunction below.

1. and _____

_____

2. so _____

_____

3. but _____

_____

Students write routinely for a range of tasks, purposes, and audiences. Students practice various conventions of standard English.

Name _____

Prefixes *un-, re-, mis-, dis-, non-*

DIRECTIONS Add the prefix *un-, re-, mis-, dis-,* or *non-* to each base word. Write the new word on the line.

1. un + load = _____

2. re + learn = _____

3. mis + direct = _____

4. dis + like = _____

5. non + sense = _____

DIRECTIONS Write the word from the Word Bank that best fits each definition.

Word Bank

nonstop	dishonest	misspell	rewrite	unknown

_____ **6.** to spell incorrectly

_____ **7.** without stopping

_____ **8.** not known

_____ **9.** to write again

_____ **10.** not truthful

DIRECTIONS Add the prefix *un-, re-, mis-,* or *dis-* to the word in parentheses to complete each sentence. Write the new word on the line.

_____ **11.** Last night I was (able) to see the stars.

_____ **12.** They seem to have (appeared) in the cloudy sky.

_____ **13.** Anyway, someone has (placed) our telescope.

_____ **14.** When I asked who used it last, no one could (call).

_____ **15.** Tonight is cloudy, so it is (likely) the stars will be out.

Students apply grade-level phonics and word analysis skills.

Name _____

DIRECTIONS Write a sentence using each word.

townhouses   suburbs   apartments   concrete   streetcars

_____

_____

_____

_____

_____

_____

_____

Write in Response to Reading

Think about the different types of homes described in *City Homes*. Which type of home would you want to live in? State your opinion and support it with text evidence.

_____

_____

_____

_____

_____

Students demonstrate contextual understanding of Benchmark Vocabulary. Students read text closely and use text evidence in their written answers.

Name _____

Conveying Ideas and Information Choose a topic and write an informative/explanatory paragraph about it. Your paragraph should express your views about the topic while providing factual information.

_____

_____

_____

_____

_____

Review the Definition of Adverbs

DIRECTIONS Circle the adverb(s) in each sentence, and underline the word that it modifies. Then identify whether the word it modifies is a verb, adjective, or adverb.

1. The soup is very hot. _____

2. Margaret ate her lunch slowly. _____

3. Victor walked too quickly. _____

Students write routinely for a range of tasks, purposes, and audiences. Students practice various conventions of standard English.

Name _____

DIRECTIONS Write a sentence using each word.

townhouses   suburbs   apartments

_____

_____

_____

Write in Response to Reading

Read the "School and play" section of *City Homes*. Write an informative paragraph describing some of the things people can do for entertainment in a city.

_____

_____

_____

_____

_____

Students demonstrate contextual understanding of Benchmark Vocabulary. Students read text closely and use text evidence in their written answers.

Name _____

Literal and Nonliteral Meanings

DIRECTIONS Using evidence from the text, answer the following questions about page 113 of *City Homes*.

1. What is the meaning of the word *cold* as it is used on page 113? Is this a literal or nonliteral meaning of the word?

   _____

   _____

2. If the word *cold* has a literal meaning on page 113, what is a nonliteral meaning of the word? If the word *cold* has a nonliteral meaning on page 113, what is a literal meaning of the word?

   _____

   _____

   _____

3. What is the meaning of the word *warm* as it is used on page 113? Is this a literal or nonliteral meaning of the word?

   _____

   _____

   _____

4. If the word *warm* has a literal meaning on page 113, what is a nonliteral meaning of the word? If the word *warm* has a nonliteral meaning on page 113, what is a literal meaning of the word?

   _____

   _____

Students analyze and respond to literary and informational text.

Name _____

Understanding Different Genres On a separate sheet of paper, complete a Web B graphic organizer to compare and contrast three genres of informative writing: procedural writing, report writing, and explanatory writing. Place "Informative Writing" in the center oval and "Procedural Writing," "Report Writing," and "Explanatory Writing" in the outer ovals. In each oval, write the features of that genre. Then write 2–4 sentences that explain how the three genres of writing are similar and different on the lines below.

_____

_____

_____

_____

_____

_____

Conventions

Review How Adverbs Function in a Sentence

DIRECTIONS Underline the adverb in each sentence. Then tell which word it modifies, the type of word it modifies, and what sort of information it adds to the sentence.

1. Traffic moves slowly during rush hour. _____

_____

2. We drove to Milwaukee yesterday. _____

_____

3. The engine in my car is very hot. _____

_____

Students write routinely for a range of tasks, purposes, and audiences. Students practice various conventions of standard English.

Name _____

DIRECTIONS Write a sentence using each word.

concrete   streetcars

_____

_____

_____

_____

Write in Response to Reading

Read the section of *City Homes* titled "The weather." The author shows photographs of buildings in different climates. Are the photographs effective? State your opinion. Then use evidence from the text to support it.

_____

_____

_____

_____

_____

Students demonstrate contextual understanding of Benchmark Vocabulary. Students read text closely and use text evidence in their written answers.

Name _____

A Visit to Cuba

"We're going to visit Grandma!" Manny exclaimed to his little brother Leon.

"I wonder if Cuba is anything like New York City." Leon said.

Traveling to Cuba took several hours. The boys were excited to finally spot the island of Cuba outside the airplane window. On the taxi ride to Grandma's house, they got a glimpse of the city of Old Havana. The city was busy just like New York City. The honking horns made the boys feel at home.

The next day Grandmother took them to see some of her favorite places. The market had vegetables that were unusual to the boys. They enjoyed eating lunch at a restaurant outside under some tall palm trees. Colorful birds sang loudly overhead. After lunch they toured the city to see some of its biggest buildings.

"New York City has much taller buildings," thought Leon.

They stopped to listen to a band playing local instruments. Manny danced to the beat of the bongo drums.

After a week of fun, the visit had come to an end. The boys stood at the door to say goodbye. Grandmother said, "I have some gifts for you. They will help you remember your trip to Cuba." Leon unwrapped a special whistle that made sounds just like the songs the birds had sung at the restaurant. Manny opened a box with a set of bongo drums. "Now New York City can sound a little more like Cuba," laughed Grandmother.

Students read text closely to determine what the text says.

Name _____

Gather Evidence Underline the details in the story that help you to learn about life in Old Havana.

Gather Evidence: Extend Your Ideas Work with a partner, and discuss how important these details are to the story. Write 2–3 sentences explaining how important they are.

_____

_____

_____

Ask Questions What questions would you ask the boys about the trip to Cuba? Are they discussed in the text? If so, circle that section of the text.

_____

_____

Ask Questions: Extend Your Ideas What question would you ask the boys about the trip to Cuba that is not answered in the text? Research your question and write 1–2 sentences discussing it.

_____

_____

Make Your Case Do you think Old Havana and New York City have more similarities or differences? Underline key words or phrases that help answer the question.

Make Your Case: Extend Your Ideas Research New York City and Old Havana. Using the information you find, write 2–3 sentences about how they are similar and different. Discuss your results with a partner.

_____

_____

_____

Students read text closely to determine what the text says.

Name _____

Write a Description of Graphics Describe and analyze a photograph, using evidence from the text and the photograph to show how geography influences a way of life. Write a few sentences that describe the details in the photograph and a few sentences that explain what these details tell about how geography influences life.

_____

_____

_____

_____

_____

_____

Conventions

Review Using Adverbs in a Sentence

DIRECTIONS Write a sentence using each adverb below.

1. politely _____

2. never _____

3. quite _____

Students write routinely for a range of tasks, purposes, and audiences. Students practice various conventions of standard English.

Name _____

DIRECTIONS Write a sentence using each word.

similar   characters   extreme

_____

_____

_____

_____

Write in Response to Reading

Describe the similarities between the places where most people live. Why do you think most people live in places with those characteristics? Use text evidence in your response.

_____

_____

_____

_____

_____

Students demonstrate contextual understanding of Benchmark Vocabulary. Students read text closely and use text evidence in their written answers.

Name _____

Main Idea

DIRECTIONS Using evidence from the text, answer the following questions about pages 4–5 from *Deep Down and Other Extreme Places to Live.*

1. How much of the world's population lives in or near a city?

_____

_____

2. What main idea does this detail help develop?

_____

_____

3. Which types of places cover a lot of Earth?

_____

_____

4. What main idea does this detail help develop?

_____

_____

5. Why might these places be "extreme" places to live?

_____

_____

Students analyze and respond to literary and informational text.

Name _____

Introduce a Topic Write an introduction to a topic that appears in *Deep Down and Other Extreme Places to Live,* such as deserts.

_____

_____

_____

_____

_____

_____

Conventions

Review Using Coordinating Conjunctions in a Sentence

DIRECTIONS Use each coordinating conjunction below in a sentence. Then explain how it links ideas, contrasts ideas, or offers a choice.

1. or _____

_____

_____

_____

2. but _____

_____

_____

3. and _____

_____

_____

Name _____

DIRECTIONS Write a sentence using each word.

canyon   emerald   survive

_____

_____

_____

_____

_____

Write in Response to Reading

On page 6 the author uses the word *spectacular* to describe the waterfalls near Supai. Look at the image of Havasu Falls on page 11. How would you describe the falls? How does this photograph help you understand the meaning of *spectacular*?

_____

_____

_____

_____

_____

Students demonstrate contextual understanding of Benchmark Vocabulary. Students read text closely and use text evidence in their written answers.

Name _____

Develop a Topic Develop the topic you introduced in Lesson 4 by adding one or more paragraphs with facts, definitions, and details. Use the lines below or a separate sheet of paper.

_____

_____

_____

_____

_____

_____

Conventions

Define Subordinating Conjunctions

DIRECTIONS Underline the subordinate clause in each sentence. Then circle the subordinating conjunction.

1. When I finish my lunch, I will go outside and play with my friends.

2. Bruce is sad because he lost his favorite toy.

3. Lisa's parents will pick her up after they leave the movie theater.

Students write routinely for a range of tasks, purposes, and audiences. Students practice various conventions of standard English.

Name _____

Spellings of /j/, /s/, and /k/

DIRECTIONS Underline the letter or letters that stand for the **/j/ sound** as in *jar*. Then write a sentence using each word.

1. gentle _____

2. bridge _____

3. banjo _____

4. village _____

DIRECTIONS Circle the words in the Word Bank that have the **/k/ sound** spelled *k, c, ck,* and *ch*. Write the words on the lines.

Word Bank

brake	branch	cellar	salad	merchant
peaceful	anchor	dresser	pluck	concrete

5. _____

6. _____

7. _____

8. _____

DIRECTIONS Circle the words in the Word Bank that have the **/s/ sound** as in *person* or *pencil*. Write the words on the lines.

9. _____

10. _____

11. _____

12. _____

Students apply grade-level phonics and word analysis skills.

Name _____

DIRECTIONS Write a sentence using the word.

mine

_____

_____

_____

_____

Write in Response to Reading

Why is the Danakil Depression an extreme place to live? Use text evidence to support your answer.

_____

_____

_____

_____

_____

Students demonstrate contextual understanding of Benchmark Vocabulary. Students read text closely and use text evidence in their written answers.

Name _____

Use Illustrations to Aid Comprehension Find or draw illustrations for the topic you started writing about in Lesson 4, and then write captions for each one. If you find illustrations, attach them to this page, and write your captions below. If you draw illustrations, use a separate sheet of paper for your drawings and captions.

_____

_____

_____

_____

_____

Conventions

Use Subordinating Conjunctions in a Sentence

DIRECTIONS Combine each pair of sentences below using a subordinating conjunction.

1. We looked in the cupboard. Mom hides a bag of cookies there.

_____

_____

2. Aunt Martha went to the store. She made dinner for us.

_____

_____

Students write routinely for a range of tasks, purposes, and audiences. Students practice various conventions of standard English.

Name _____

DIRECTIONS Write a sentence using each word.

evaporated   provide   herd

_____

_____

_____

_____

Write in Response to Reading

How do you think you would feel if you were one of the Afar people?
Explain your answer using evidence from the text.

_____

_____

_____

_____

_____

Students demonstrate contextual
understanding of Benchmark Vocabulary.
Students read text closely and use text
evidence in their written answers.

Name _____

Main Idea and Key Details

DIRECTIONS Using evidence from the text, answer the following questions about pages 14–17 from *Deep Down and Other Extreme Places to Live*.

1. Why is salt important to the Afar people?

_____

_____

2. What sort of homes do the Afar people live in? How are these homes suited to their lifestyle?

_____

_____

3. Which two animals are especially important to the Afar people and why?

_____

_____

4. How do these details help develop a main idea?

_____

_____

_____

_____

Students analyze and respond to literary and informational text.

Name _____

Group Related Information Group related facts and key details about your topic. You can group this information by writing a paragraph below, creating lists on a separate sheet of paper, or completing a Main Idea organizer on a separate sheet of paper.

_____

_____

_____

_____

_____

Conventions

Review Plural Verbs

DIRECTIONS Rewrite each sentence using a plural subject, and change the verb to agree with the new subject.

1. She walks a long way to get home. _____

_____

2. He listens to the radio at night. _____

_____

3. It changes every month. _____

_____

Students write routinely for a range of tasks, purposes, and audiences. Students practice various conventions of standard English.

Name _____

DIRECTIONS Write a sentence using each word.

roaming   farthest

_____
_____
_____
_____

Write in Response to Reading

How do the images on pages 18 and 19 help you better understand the text? Use evidence from the text in your response.

_____
_____
_____
_____
_____
_____

Students demonstrate contextual understanding of Benchmark Vocabulary. Students read text closely and use text evidence in their written answers.

Name _____

Use Illustrations to Understand Text

DIRECTIONS Using evidence from the text, answer the following questions about pages 18–19 from *Deep Down and Other Extreme Places to Live.*

1. Look at the image on the left side of page 18. What does it show?

   _____

   _____

2. What does this help you understand about how and why the Sami people use reindeer to pull sleds?

   _____

   _____

3. Look at the image in the bottom right corner of page 19. What does it show?

   _____

   _____

4. How does this image help you understand what a summer day is like for the Sami people?

   _____

   _____

   _____

Students analyze and respond to literary and informational text.

Name _____

Use Linking Words to Connect Ideas Write a paragraph using linking words and phrases to connect ideas.

_____

_____

_____

_____

_____

_____

Conventions

Use Regular Verbs

DIRECTIONS Complete each sentence with the correct form of the regular verb.

1. I _____ (look) at my little brother.

2. He _____ (ask) my parents for permission to go to his room.

3. They _____ (allow) him to leave the table.

Students write routinely for a range of tasks, purposes, and audiences. Students practice various conventions of standard English.

Name _____

DIRECTIONS Write a sentence using each word.

species   occasions

_____

_____

_____

_____

Write in Response to Reading

Look at the text box on page 21. What do the headings help you understand about the Sami people's use of reindeer?

_____

_____

_____

_____

_____

Students demonstrate contextual understanding of Benchmark Vocabulary. Students read text closely and use text evidence in their written answers.

Name _____

Use Linking Words to Connect Ideas Write a paragraph using linking
words and phrases to compare and contrast two kinds of extreme
communities or two things people do in an extreme community.

_____

_____

_____

_____

_____

_____

Conventions

Use Plural Subjects and Verbs

DIRECTIONS Write a sentence using each verb in the present tense with
a plural subject.

1. keep _____

2. throw _____

3. stop _____

Students write routinely for a range of
tasks, purposes, and audiences. Students
practice various conventions of standard
English.

Name _____

DIRECTIONS Write a sentence using each word.

probably   imagine   normal

_____

_____

_____

_____

Write in Response to Reading

Do you think that your life might seem extreme to the people you read about in *Deep Down and Other Extreme Places to Live?* Explain your answer using evidence from the text.

_____

_____

_____

_____

_____

Students demonstrate contextual understanding of Benchmark Vocabulary. Students read text closely and use text evidence in their written answers.

Name _____

Provide a Concluding Statement or Section Write a paragraph that concludes the piece of informative writing that you started in Lesson 4.

_____

_____

_____

_____

_____

_____

Conventions

Review Regular Past-Tense Verbs

DIRECTIONS Complete each sentence with the correct past-tense form of the verb.

1. My mother _____ (help) her friend move yesterday.

2. Melissa and I _____ (pack) a few boxes.

3. Then my mother and her friend _____ (label) each one.

Students write routinely for a range of tasks, purposes, and audiences. Students practice various conventions of standard English.

Name _____

Suffixes *-ly, -ful, -ness, -less, -able, -ible*

DIRECTIONS Add the suffix *-ly, -ful, -ness, -able, -ible,* or *-less* to each base word. Write the new word on the line.

1. grace + ful = _____

2. bare + ly = _____

3. depend + able = _____

4. fair + ness = _____

5. digest + ible = _____

6. wire + less = _____

7. rare + ly = _____

8. neat + ness = _____

DIRECTIONS Add the suffix *-ly, -ful, -ness, -able, -ible,* or *-less* to the base word in parentheses to complete each sentence. You may have to make a slight spelling change. Write the new word on the line.

_____ 9. A (care) mistake can cause a spill.

_____ 10. A spill can (quick) lead to falls.

_____ 11. We can all help by being (response).

_____ 12. If you see a spill, (safe) mop it up.

_____ 13. Be (care) to blockade any wet area.

_____ 14. Your (thoughtful) will be appreciated.

_____ 15. The area will be (pass) again in no time.

Students apply grade-level phonics and word analysis skills.

Name _____

DIRECTIONS Write a sentence using the word.

medicinal

_____

_____

_____

_____

Write in Response to Reading

DIRECTIONS Read the definitions included in the glossary on page 26. Select one or two words, and explain how each definition helps you better understand an idea in the text.

_____

_____

_____

_____

_____

_____

Students demonstrate contextual understanding of Benchmark Vocabulary. Students read text closely and use text evidence in their written answers.

Name _____

Take Brief Notes on Sources Choose a topic from the list provided by your teacher. Research it, take notes on the sources you find, and write down definitions of unknown words. Write those notes and definitions below or on a separate sheet of paper.

_____

_____

_____

_____

_____

_____

Use Regular Past-Tense Verbs in a Sentence

DIRECTIONS Write a sentence using each verb in the past tense and with the type of subject identified.

1. fill (singular subject) _____

   _____

2. fill (plural subject) _____

   _____

3. save (singular subject) _____

   _____

4. save (plural subject) _____

   _____

Students write routinely for a range of tasks, purposes, and audiences. Students practice various conventions of standard English.

Name _____

DIRECTIONS Write a sentence using each word.

cities   similar   normal

_____

_____

_____

_____

Write in Response to Reading

Compare and contrast one type of home from *City Homes* and one type of home from *Deep Down and Other Extreme Places to Live.* How are the homes appropriate for living in a certain place? Write your answer below, on a separate sheet of paper, or in a new document.

_____

_____

_____

_____

_____

_____

Students demonstrate contextual
understanding of Benchmark Vocabulary.
Students read text closely and use text
evidence in their written answers.

Name _____

Compare and Contrast

DIRECTIONS Using evidence from the texts, answer the following questions about *City Homes* and *Deep Down and Other Extreme Places to Live.*

1. *Deep Down and Other Extreme Places to Live* shows how people who live in extreme places overcome many challenges to live there. What challenges do people face in *City Homes,* and how do they overcome them?

   _____

   _____

   _____

   _____

2. What are some advantages and disadvantages of living in a big city?

   _____

   _____

   _____

3. What are some advantages and disadvantages of living in a small town or village?

   _____

   _____

   _____

4. Could any of the places from *Deep Down and Other Extreme Places to Live* be included in *City Homes*? Could any places in *City Homes* be included in *Deep Down and Other Extreme Places to Live*? Support your answer with evidence from the text.

   _____

   _____

Students analyze and respond to literary and informational text.

Name _____

Gather Information On a separate sheet of paper, write a paragraph about the topic you chose in Lesson 11. Use your notes from the previous lesson, as well as facts, details, and definitions from three sources to develop your paragraph. You may use *City Homes* and *Deep Down and Other Extreme Places to Live* as two of your sources. List your sources after the end of your paragraph.

Conventions

Define Plural Irregular Verbs

DIRECTIONS Fill in the blanks by writing the past-tense form of each verb in parentheses.

1. They _____ (build) the house last year.

2. We _____ (make) collages in art class.

3. My sisters _____ (become) very quiet.

Students write routinely for a range of tasks, purposes, and audiences. Students practice various conventions of standard English.

Benchmark Vocabulary

Name _____

DIRECTIONS Write a sentence using each word.

journey   shuffled   crooked   drought

_____

_____

_____

_____

Write in Response to Reading

Traditions, songs, beliefs, and stories make up a culture's folklore. How can folklore do more than entertain people? Use examples from the text and your own experience to support your answer.

_____

_____

_____

_____

_____

Students demonstrate contextual understanding of Benchmark Vocabulary. Students read text closely and use text evidence in their written answers.

Name _____

The World's Smallest Nation

What would it be like to live on an island in the Pacific Ocean that is only about 8 square miles? How is living on an island community different? How does it affect the culture? You might ask someone who lives on the Republic of Nauru (nah-OO-roo).

Nauru sits just south of the equator. Its closest neighbor is a whopping 200 miles away! About 3,000 years ago, the first people migrated to the island from Micronesia and Polynesia. They lived in tribes or groups much like the Native Americans of North America did. Nauru had a unique culture and enjoyed peace for centuries.

In 1798, a British captain of a whaling ship saw Nauru on his way to China. Later, the first Europeans arrived. They brought new ideas, weapons, and war. From the 1800s to the mid-1900s, different European countries, Japan, and Australia took control of Nauru. They used its resources for trade and influenced Nauru's culture and community. Finally, Nauru gained its freedom in 1968.

Today, Nauru is home to many different cultures because of its history. More than half of the people speak the Nauruan language. English is also spoken, but less than 10 percent of the people are European. Other groups include Pacific Islanders and Chinese. As an independent nation, Nauru's culture is still unique. Its culture is traditional with a blend of other cultures from around the world.

Name _____

Gather Evidence What additional information can you learn from the pictures and labels? Circle information from the text that corresponds with the pictures and labels.

_____

_____

Gather Evidence: Extend Your Ideas Write a sentence explaining how the pictures contribute to what is conveyed by the text.

_____

_____

Ask Questions What questions would you ask someone who had visited Nauru? Circle information in the text that answers these questions.

_____

_____

Ask Questions: Extend Your Ideas What questions would you ask someone who had visited Nauru that are not answered in the text? Research your questions and write 1–2 sentences discussing each one.

_____

_____

Make Your Case What are two interesting differences between Nauru and where you live? Why do you think those differences are interesting?

_____

_____

Make Your Case: Extend Your Ideas Write 2–3 sentences using information you researched about Nauru and comparing it to where you live. Discuss your results with a partner.

_____

_____

_____

Students read text closely to determine what the text says.

Writing

Name _____

Sort Evidence Sort evidence for an essay that will compare your own way of life to the research you have done on other communities. Sort your notes from Lessons 11 and 12 into at least three categories. Use the space below or a separate sheet of paper.

_____

_____

_____

_____

_____

_____

Conventions

How Plural Irregular Verbs Function

DIRECTIONS Rewrite each sentence below in the past tense.

1. They run five miles every day. _____

_____

2. Myra and Frank are outside. _____

_____

3. Felix and Thomas go to practice every Tuesday. _____

_____

Students write routinely for a range of tasks, purposes, and audiences. Students practice various conventions of standard English.

Name _____

DIRECTIONS Write a sentence using each word.

desert   limit   navigate   celebrate

_____

_____

_____

_____

_____

Write in Response to Reading

Did Ramata want Grandma to go with her? Why or why not? Use evidence from the text to support your answer.

_____

_____

_____

_____

_____

_____

Students demonstrate contextual understanding of Benchmark Vocabulary. Students read text closely and use text evidence in their written answers.

Name _____

Plan and Prewrite Create an outline for your essay comparing and contrasting your way of life with the way of life in other communities. First, use print and reliable digital sources to gather additional information. Then, use this information and the information you collected in Lessons 11–13 to make an outline for an essay. Write your outline on a separate sheet of paper.

Conventions

Use Plural Irregular Verbs in a Sentence

DIRECTIONS Write a sentence using each irregular verb in the past tense with a plural subject.

1. get _____

2. catch _____

3. eat _____

Students write routinely for a range of tasks, purposes, and audiences. Students practice various conventions of standard English.

Name _____

DIRECTIONS Write a sentence using each word.

natural   spring

_____

_____

_____

_____

Write in Response to Reading

Find an unfamiliar word in the text. Write what you think the word means and what clues in the text helped you come up with that definition. Then explain how this word adds meaning to the story.

_____

_____

_____

_____

_____

Students demonstrate contextual
understanding of Benchmark Vocabulary.
Students read text closely and use text
evidence in their written answers.

Name _____

Determine Word Meaning

DIRECTIONS Using evidence from the text, answer the following questions about *The Song of Sky and Sand.*

1. What does *drowned out* mean on page 8?

   _____

2. What clues in the text help you understand the meaning of *drowned out?* Explain how they help you understand the word's meaning.

   _____

   _____

   _____

   _____

   _____

3. What does *cry* mean in the second sentence on page 33? What does *cries* mean in the last sentence on page 36?

   _____

4. What clues in the text help you understand the meaning of *cry* on page 33? Explain how they help you understand its meaning.

   _____

   _____

   _____

5. What clues in the text help you understand the meaning of *cries* on page 36? Explain how they help you understand its meaning.

   _____

   _____

Students analyze and respond to literary and informational text.

Name _____

Draft an Essay Use the outline you made in Lesson 14 to draft a compare-and-contrast essay about your way of life and the way of life in other communities. Write your draft on a separate sheet of paper.

Use Past-Tense Irregular Verbs in a Sentence

DIRECTIONS Write a sentence using each verb in the past tense.

1. give _____

2. spring _____

3. know _____

Students write routinely for a range of tasks, purposes, and audiences. Students practice various conventions of standard English.

Name _____

Consonant Patterns *wr, kn, gn, st, mb*

DIRECTIONS Choose the word in parentheses with the silent consonant, as in *wr, kn, st, mb,* or *gn,* to complete each sentence. Write the word on the line.

_____ 1. It was a perfect winter day for a (climb/hike).

_____ 2. Theo packed water and snacks in a (cooler/knapsack).

_____ 3. Brin handed Theo a (knit/new) cap.

_____ 4. She grabbed the scarf with the zigzag (checks/design).

_____ 5. She (wrapped/threw) another scarf around Theo's neck.

_____ 6. Theo began (fastening/dusting) the snaps on his jacket.

_____ 7. Then someone said, "(Listen/Answer) to the radio!"

_____ 8. There were (signs/signals) that a big storm was coming.

_____ 9. Theo and Brin (knew/realized) their plans had to change.

DIRECTIONS Circle each word in the Word Bank that has a silent consonant. Write the circled words in alphabetical order on the lines below.

Word Bank

gnaw	relax	castle	wriggle	basket	water
trap	numb	next	comb	knot	humid

10. _____   13. _____

11. _____   14. _____

12. _____   15. _____

Students apply grade-level phonics and word analysis skills.

Name _____

DIRECTIONS Write a sentence using each word.

extreme   journey

_____

_____

_____

_____

Write a paragraph comparing and contrasting how people use animals to survive in each of the texts.

_____

_____

_____

_____

_____

Students demonstrate contextual understanding of Benchmark Vocabulary. Students read text closely and use text evidence in their written answers.

Name _____

Revise an Essay On a separate sheet of paper, make revisions to your compare-and-contrast essay from Lesson 15. Look for information you left out or may want to cut from your essay.

Conventions

Use Conventional Spelling

DIRECTIONS For each word and suffix combination, spell the word they create correctly.

Example: swim + ing = <u>swimming</u>.

1. mop + ed = _____

2. hope + ful = _____

3. salty + ness = _____

Students write routinely for a range of tasks, purposes, and audiences. Students practice various conventions of standard English.

Name _____

DIRECTIONS Write a sentence using each word.

townhouses   suburbs   apartments   desert

_____

_____

_____

_____

_____

Write in Response to Reading

Think about how the illustrations in *The Song of Sky and Sand* and the photographs in *City Homes* helped you understand the text. Did you find the illustrations in *The Song of Sky and Sand* or the photographs in *City Homes* more useful? Explain your answer using evidence from the texts.

_____

_____

_____

_____

_____

Students demonstrate contextual understanding of Benchmark Vocabulary. Students read text closely and use text evidence in their written answers.

Edit an Essay Find a partner, and then trade and edit each other's compare-and-contrast essays. Look for errors in spelling, grammar, and punctuation. Also note places where the wording is awkward and where more or different details might improve the writing. Mark any errors or suggestions in a different colored pen or pencil, and discuss them with your partner.

Use Spelling Patterns and Generalizations

DIRECTIONS Circle the correctly spelled word in parentheses.

1. I saw a lot of (monkeys / monkeies) at the zoo.

2. (Pik / Pick) fresh ingredients at the market.

3. She (trys / tries) to study for an hour every night.

Students write routinely for a range of tasks, purposes, and audiences. Students practice various conventions of standard English.

Name _____

DIRECTIONS Write a sentence using each word.

provide   concrete   streetcars

_____

_____

_____

_____

Write in Response to Reading

How have *City Homes, Deep Down and Other Extreme Places to Live,* and *The Song of Sky and Sand* helped you understand the similarities and differences between the communities of the world? Use evidence from the texts to support your answer.

_____

_____

_____

_____

Students demonstrate contextual understanding of Benchmark Vocabulary. Students read text closely and use text evidence in their written answers.

Name _____

Compare and Contrast

DIRECTIONS Using evidence from the texts, answer the following
questions about *City Homes, Deep Down and Other Extreme Places to
Live*, and *The Song of Sky and Sand*.

1. How does each text show the connection between people's
   surroundings and their culture?

   _____

   _____

   _____

2. Which two communities from the three texts have the most
   similarities? Explain your answer using evidence from the texts.

   _____

   _____

   _____

3. Which two communities from the three texts have the most
   differences? Explain your answer using evidence from the texts.

   _____

   _____

   _____

4. Which text was the most interesting to read? Explain your answer
   using evidence from the text.

   _____

   _____

   _____

Students analyze and respond to literary
and informational text.

Name _____

Publish and Present Your Writing Write an edited version of your compare-and-contrast essay on a separate sheet of paper. Then publish your compare-and-contrast essay and present it to the class.

Consult Reference Materials to Check Words

DIRECTIONS Read the following sentences, and use reference materials to check the spelling of each underlined word. Write *correct* on the line if the word is spelled correctly, and identify the source you used to check the spelling. If the spelling is incorrect, write the correct spelling, and identify the source you used to check the spelling.

1. <u>Soul</u> is the capital of South Korea. _____

2. Gumbo is a traditional <u>Creole</u> dish. _____

3. Lauren had a bad <u>atitude</u>, so no one talked to her. _____

Students write routinely for a range of tasks, purposes, and audiences. Students practice various conventions of standard English.

Name _____

Irregular Plurals

DIRECTIONS Use the plural form of each word in parentheses to complete each sentence. Write the word on the line.

_____ **1.** Timmy wasn't like the other (mouse).

_____ **2.** He was missing all his (tooth).

_____ **3.** He couldn't chew the (loaf) of bread.

_____ **4.** Using his (foot) to tear off small pieces took too long.

_____ **5.** Of course, the (woman) would not help him.

_____ **6.** Timmy hid from the cleaning (man), too.

_____ **7.** At last, Timmy saw (child) dropping crumbs.

_____ **8.** Now he stores crumbs on (shelf), to eat whenever he wants.

DIRECTIONS Write the plural form of each word below.

9. wife _____   **15.** deer _____

10. wolf _____   **16.** elf _____

11. scarf _____   **17.** half _____

12. hero _____   **18.** goose _____

13. cuff _____   **19.** knife _____

14. calf _____   **20.** sheep _____

Students apply grade-level phonics and word analysis skills.

Name _____

DIRECTIONS Write a sentence using the word.

canyon

_____

_____

_____

_____

Write in Response to Reading

Read pages 7–11. Keep in mind the order of events of the story the grandfather tells the boy. Write an explanatory paragraph that summarizes how the characters contributed to the sequence of events in the excerpt. Keep the events in the order they appear in the text.

_____

_____

_____

_____

_____

Students demonstrate contextual understanding of Benchmark Vocabulary. Students read text closely and use text evidence in their written answers.

Name _____

Contributions of Illustrations to a Text

DIRECTIONS Using evidence from the text, answer the following questions about pages 6–11 of *Knots on a Counting Rope.*

1. What does the illustration on pages 6–7 tell you about the characters that the text does not?

   _____

   _____

2. How do the characters feel on pages 8–9? What clues in the illustration support your opinion?

   _____

   _____

3. On page 11, what does it say the great blue horses gave the boy? How does the illustration help show that information?

   _____

   _____

   _____

Students analyze and respond to literary and informational text.

Name _____

State an Opinion Think about a topic you feel strongly about. Write a paragraph in which you present your opinion and give reasons and examples that support your opinion.

_____

_____

_____

_____

_____

_____

Conventions

Function of Nouns

DIRECTIONS Underline the noun that serves as the subject of the sentence. Then identify whether the noun names a person, place, animal, or thing.

1. The orange cat leapt from the cold, hard floor to the soft, warm bed. _____

2. Two yellow buses drove down the road toward the school. _____

3. Julia is watching her children from the window. _____

Students write routinely for a range of tasks, purposes, and audiences. Students practice various conventions of standard English.

Name _____

DIRECTIONS Write a sentence using each word.

ceremony   sweep

_____

_____

_____

_____

Write in Response to Reading

Reread pages 12–16 of *Knots on a Counting Rope*. Write an explanatory paragraph that touches on the literal and nonliteral uses of words and phrases on those pages. Use the vocabulary words and evidence from the text to support your writing.

_____

_____

_____

_____

_____

Students demonstrate contextual understanding of Benchmark Vocabulary. Students read text closely and use text evidence in their written answers.

Name _____

Write About Reading On a separate sheet of paper, write a short opinion essay about *Knots on a Counting Rope*. State an opinion about the book, state an opinion about one or both of the characters, and support your opinions with reasons and examples from the text.

Conventions

Function of Nouns in Sentences

DIRECTIONS Circle the nouns in each sentence. Tell whether each noun is the subject, direct object, or indirect object of the sentence.

1. Cho quickly threw the baseball.

_____

_____

2. Sarah sent Amare an e-mail.

_____

_____

3. Nate cooked dinner.

_____

_____

Students write routinely for a range of tasks, purposes, and audiences. Students practice various conventions of standard English.

Benchmark Vocabulary

Name _____

DIRECTIONS Write a sentence using each word.

traced   surround

_____

_____

_____

_____

Write in Response to Reading

Read page 20 of *Knots on a Counting Rope*. Write a paragraph that touches on the literal and nonliteral uses of words and phrases on this page. Use the vocabulary words and evidence from the text to support your writing.

_____

_____

_____

_____

_____

_____

Students demonstrate contextual
understanding of Benchmark Vocabulary.
Students read text closely and use text
evidence in their written answers.

We Need New Tornado Warnings!

Over 1,200 tornadoes touched down in the United States in 2010. Sirens are often used to alert people of the possibility of a tornado. I think tornado sirens are now obsolete. They should be replaced.

Obviously, it is important to warn people of danger. In the past, bells were hung high in towers to warn people. When communities began to use electricity in the 1930s, sirens replaced bells as the warning signal.

I grew up listening to the blares of tornado siren tests. They happened every Wednesday morning at 10:00. Clear, sunny days in the summer were suddenly interrupted with a deafening siren. I got used to ignoring them.

Also, tornado sirens can cause panic in people who aren't used to them. One time, a visitor heard the Wednesday morning siren test. She panicked. She ran inside for shelter. There was not a rain cloud in sight. Such is the power of a tornado siren!

There are better ways to warn people about tornadoes. By the 1960s, radio and television were used as warning systems. With the Internet, cell phones, and smartphones, we now have fast ways of tracking a storm. This technology can even help you locate the nearest tornado shelter! With a siren, you have only a warning and not much else.

Finally, sirens can cost lots of money. Let's spend the money we save from not using sirens on sharing information. We can make certain that emergency weather information is communicated through the technology of today.

Students read text closely to determine what the text says.

Name _____

Gather Evidence Circle the clues in the text that tell you the writer is giving both facts and opinions.

Gather Evidence: Extend Your Ideas Did you circle "I think"? Explain why this is a good opinion clue.

_____

_____

Ask Questions Underline two observations the narrator makes about siren tests. What two questions would you ask an expert about tornado warnings?

_____

_____

Ask Questions: Extend Your Ideas What would you ask someone who has survived a tornado?

_____

_____

Make Your Case Do you think the writer does a good job of stating an opinion and giving reasons to support it? Underline examples from the text that support your opinion about the writer's skills.

_____

_____

Make Your Case: Extend Your Ideas On a separate piece of paper, write at least 3–4 sentences stating your opinions about the writer's skills. Make sure to give reasons to support it. Trade papers with a partner and discuss what you have written.

Students read text closely to determine what the text says.

Name _____

Writing About the Unit Topic Write an opinion about the relationship between the grandfather and grandson in *Knots on a Counting Rope*. Support your opinion with reasons and evidence from the text.

_____

_____

_____

_____

_____

Functions of Pronouns

DIRECTIONS Underline the pronoun in each sentence. Then write whether the pronoun is the subject, direct object, or indirect object of the sentence.

1. Lily bought me a book. _____

_____

2. She said the book was really interesting. _____

_____

3. Lily's mother likes it too. _____

_____

Students write routinely for a range of tasks, purposes, and audiences. Students practice various conventions of standard English.

Name _____

DIRECTIONS Write a sentence using each word.

canyon   traced

_____

_____

_____

_____

Write in Response to Reading

Read pages 17–18 of *Knots on a Counting Rope*. Write a paragraph that explains the boy's traits, motivations, and feelings.

_____

_____

_____

_____

_____

_____

Students demonstrate contextual understanding of Benchmark Vocabulary. Students read text closely and use text evidence in their written answers.

Name _____

Introduce a Topic Write a few sentences introducing this topic: How can relationships between people in different generations have an impact on a person's life?

_____

_____

_____

_____

_____

_____

Use Pronouns as Sentence Subjects

DIRECTIONS In each pair of sentences below, circle the pronoun that serves as the subject of a sentence. Then underline the noun(s) the pronoun replaces.

1. The sugar was not in the pantry. It was on the kitchen counter.

2. Rhonda and Brian are driving from Maryland to Oregon. They will stop and visit museums along the way.

3. Melissa will not stay with her aunt this summer. She will work at the mall.

Students write routinely for a range of tasks, purposes, and audiences. Students practice various conventions of standard English.

Name _____

DIRECTIONS Write a sentence using the word.

fluttering

_____

_____

_____

_____

Write in Response to Reading

Read page 6 of the text. Do you think it's hard to imagine a grown-up as a little child? Why or why not? Use evidence from the text to support your answer.

_____

_____

_____

_____

_____

_____

 Students demonstrate contextual understanding of Benchmark Vocabulary. Students read text closely and use text evidence in their written answers.

Lesson 5

Name _____

Figurative Language

DIRECTIONS Using evidence from the text, answer the following questions about pages 9–13 from *Storm in the Night.*

1. On page 9, the narrator states, "Thomas had a chin as smooth as a peach." How does this help you understand the way Thomas's chin feels?

   _____

   _____

2. On page 9, the narrator states, "Grandfather had a voice like a tuba. Thomas's voice was like a penny whistle." What does this description mean?

   _____

   _____

3. Read page 12. The author uses the words *ping, tick,* and *bong* in her descriptions of clocks and bells. Why does the author use these words? What do they sound like?

   _____

   _____

   _____

Students analyze and respond to literary and informational text.

Name _____

State an Opinion Complete the sentences below to write four opinion statements about the topic you introduced in Lesson 4. Remember that you are writing about how relationships between people from different generations can have an impact on a person's life.

1. I like _____.

2. I do not like _____.

3. My favorite _____ is _____.

4. I like _____ better than _____.

Conventions

Use Pronouns as Objects

DIRECTIONS Circle the correct pronoun to complete each sentence.

1. Jack asked (she / her) for help lifting the box.

2. My father gave (he / him) the computer.

3. Mrs. Smith drove (they / them) to the movie theater.

Students write routinely for a range of tasks, purposes, and audiences. Students practice various conventions of standard English.

Name _____

R-Controlled Vowels *ir, er, ur, ear, or, ar, ore, oar*

DIRECTIONS Circle the words in the Word Bank that have the vowel sound /er/ as in *bird, her, turn, earn,* and *work.* Then write the words you circled under the word that has the same vowel spelling.

Word Bank

burst	hear	corn	dear	early	there	stern
fire	flare	heart	girl	hurry	learn	pear
perch	skirt	tire	torn	world	worm	

bird

1. _____

2. _____

her

3. _____

4. _____

turn

5. _____

6. _____

earn

7. _____

8. _____

work

9. _____

10. _____

DIRECTIONS Circle the word that has the same vowel sound as the first word. Then write a sentence that uses the word you circled.

11. **farm**   frame   dart   rare

_____

12. **short**   hoot   horn   shot

_____

13. **core**   cone   to   shore

_____

14. **board**   boat   proud   roar

_____

Students apply grade-level phonics and word analysis skills.

Name _____

DIRECTIONS Write a sentence using each word.

brandishing   commanded   interrupting   ashamed

_____

_____

_____

_____

_____

_____

Write in Response to Reading

Look at the illustration on page 26 and read page 27. Write an explanatory paragraph about how the illustration on page 26 contributes to the grandfather's story on page 27.

_____

_____

_____

_____

_____

Students demonstrate contextual understanding of Benchmark Vocabulary. Students read text closely and use text evidence in their written answers.

Name _____

Contributions of Illustrations to a Text

DIRECTIONS Using evidence from the text, answer the following questions about pages 16–26 from *Storm in the Night.*

1. Look at the illustration on page 16. Then read page 17. Which strong words from the text help tell about the sights and sounds of the storm around them as Thomas and his grandfather sit on the swing?

   _____

   _____

   _____

2. On page 19, what can you tell from Grandfather and Thomas's relationship by looking at how they are sitting together? Explain.

   _____

   _____

3. Read the last part of page 21 beginning with the sentence, "So there we were, the two of us, . . ." Then look at the illustration on page 22. How can readers tell that the large illustration is what Grandfather is thinking in the past?

   _____

   _____

   _____

4. How does the illustration on page 26 change the mood of the story? Which details in the illustration convey this mood?

   _____

   _____

   _____

Students analyze and respond to literary and informational text.

Name _____

Reasons to Support an Opinion Write reasons that support the four opinions you stated in Lesson 5.

_____

_____

_____

_____

_____

_____

Conventions

Functions of Adjectives

DIRECTIONS Circle the adjective in each sentence. Then underline the noun that it describes.

1. The kids ran through the dirty puddle of water.

2. The playful dog kept jumping on the sofa to get Lisa's attention.

3. New Orleans is very hot during the summer.

Students write routinely for a range of tasks, purposes, and audiences. Students practice various conventions of standard English.

Name _____

DIRECTIONS Write a sentence using the word.

mutterings

_____

_____

_____

_____

Write in Response to Reading

Write a paragraph that explains why you think the author used nonliteral meanings in the text. Use text evidence to support your answer.

_____

_____

_____

_____

_____

_____

Students demonstrate contextual understanding of Benchmark Vocabulary. Students read text closely and use text evidence in their written answers.

Name _____

Literal and Nonliteral Meanings

DIRECTIONS Using evidence from the text, answer the following questions about page 28 of *Storm in the Night*.

1. On page 28, the narrator states, "The storm was spent." What does *spent* mean in this sentence?

_____

_____

2. What words or phrases around *spent* help readers understand its meaning?

_____

_____

_____

3. Read the last paragraph on page 28. What does *mutterings* mean?

_____

_____

4. Does the author really mean that the thunder is muttering? Explain.

_____

_____

_____

Students analyze and respond to literary and informational text.

Name _____

Support an Opinion with Reasons Select one of the following opinions:

1. Bringing lunch from home is/is not better than buying it at the cafeteria.

2. *Storm in the Night* is/is not a good book for very young children.

On the lines below, write the opinion you selected, reasons that will support it, and facts and details that help explain those reasons.

_____

_____

_____

_____

_____

Conventions

Functions of Adjectives in Sentences

DIRECTIONS Rewrite each sentence, adding at least one adjective.

1. The boy walked cautiously across the bridge.

_____

2. Monica picked the flowers from her yard.

_____

3. The cat ran under the house.

_____

Students write routinely for a range of tasks, purposes, and audiences. Students practice various conventions of standard English.

Name _____

DIRECTIONS Write a sentence using each word.

fluttering   commanded

_____

_____

_____

Write in Response to Reading

Write an explanatory paragraph that summarizes the sequence of events in the story.

_____

_____

_____

_____

_____

Students demonstrate contextual
understanding of Benchmark Vocabulary.
Students read text closely and use text
evidence in their written answers.

Create an Organizational Structure Plan and organize the reasons and supporting details for an opinion piece. First, choose one of your opinion statements from Lesson 5 and the reasons that support that opinion from Lesson 6. Next, on a separate sheet of paper, take notes on evidence from the text that relates to your opinion and reasons. Then, create an outline to organize your reasons and supporting details. Finally, write your opinion essay, using your outline as a guide for structuring it.

Conventions

Use Adjectives

DIRECTIONS Write sentences that use adjectives to describe parts of *Storm in the Night*.

1. _____

   _____

2. _____

   _____

3. _____

   _____

Students write routinely for a range of tasks, purposes, and audiences. Students practice various conventions of standard English.

Name _____

DIRECTIONS Write a sentence using the word.

brandishing

_____

_____

_____

_____

Write in Response to Reading

Write a paragraph explaining whether or not you think Grandfather made the right choice in telling this story to Thomas. Use evidence from the text to support your answer.

_____

_____

_____

_____

_____

_____

Students demonstrate contextual understanding of Benchmark Vocabulary. Students read text closely and use text evidence in their written answers.

Use Linking Words and Phrases to Connect Ideas On a separate sheet of paper, add linking words and phrases to connect your opinion and reasons in the opinion piece you wrote in Lesson 8.

Conventions

Form Comparative and Superlative Adjectives

DIRECTIONS Complete each sentence with an appropriate comparative or superlative adjective.

1. Ringo's eyes were _____ than Thomas's eyes.

2. The thunder was the _____ thunder Thomas had ever heard.

3. The green coat is _____ than the blue coat.

Students write routinely for a range of tasks, purposes, and audiences. Students practice various conventions of standard English.

Name _____

DIRECTIONS Write a sentence using each word.

ceremony   interrupting

_____

_____

_____

_____

Write in Response to Reading

Read pages 18–28 in *Storm in the Night* and pages 8–13 in *Knots on a Counting Rope*. Compare and contrast the range of feelings experienced by the grandfathers in the telling of their stories. Use text evidence to support your response.

_____

_____

_____

_____

_____

_____

_____

_____

Students demonstrate contextual understanding of Benchmark Vocabulary. Students read text closely and use text evidence in their written answers.

Name _____

Provide a Concluding Statement Write a concluding statement for the opinion piece you began in Lesson 8.

_____

_____

_____

_____

_____

_____

Conventions

Using Irregular Comparatives and Superlatives

DIRECTIONS Complete each sentence with the correct form of *bad*. Explain why it is correct.

1. The last stab of lightning was the _____ of the night.

_____

_____

2. That flash of lightning was _____.

_____

_____

3. The lightning I just saw was _____ than the one I saw

earlier. _____

_____

Students write routinely for a range of tasks, purposes, and audiences. Students practice various conventions of standard English.

Name _____

Prefixes *pre-, mid-, over-, bi-, out-, de-*

DIRECTIONS Add the prefix *pre-, mid-, over-, out-,* or *de-* to each base word.

1. over- + load = _____

2. out- + going = _____

3. pre- + paid = _____

4. mid- + point = _____

5. de- + code = _____

DIRECTIONS Choose the word from the Word Bank that best fits the definition, and write the word on the line.

Word Bank

bicycle	midweek	outburst	defrost	prefix

_____ **6.** a word part added to the beginning of a word

_____ **7.** a vehicle with two wheels

_____ **8.** sudden display of emotion

_____ **9.** the middle of the week

_____ **10.** to thaw something that is frozen

DIRECTIONS Add the prefix *pre-, mid-, over-, out-,* or *bi-* to the base word in parentheses to complete each sentence. You will use each prefix just once. Write the word on the line.

_____ **11.** Elena began collecting rocks in (school).

_____ **12.** She knew this hobby would (last) any other hobby.

_____ **13.** It is easy to (look) special rocks in bright sunlight.

_____ **14.** She found a (color) rock one day, however.

_____ **15.** Finding colorful rocks at (night) is nearly impossible.

Students apply grade-level phonics and word analysis skills.

Lesson 11

Name _____

DIRECTIONS Write a sentence using each word.

hitched   stubborn

_____

_____

_____

_____

Write in Response to Reading

Read pages 26–27 from "Growing Up." Write a few sentences about your opinion on Babe and Paul becoming friends and working together. Support your writing using text evidence.

_____

_____

_____

_____

_____

Students demonstrate contextual understanding of Benchmark Vocabulary. Students read text closely and use text evidence in their written answers.

Name _____

Provide a Concluding Section Expand your concluding statement from Lesson 10 into a concluding section for your opinion piece. First, review your work, and then write a conclusion of at least three sentences that restates the main ideas of your essay (your opinion and reasons).

_____

_____

_____

_____

_____

_____

Conventions

Use Comparative and Superlative Adjectives

DIRECTIONS Write a sentence about *Paul Bunyan* with each adjective.

1. younger _____

_____

2. most powerful _____

_____

3. best _____

_____

Students write routinely for a range of tasks, purposes, and audiences. Students practice various conventions of standard English.

Name _____

DIRECTIONS Write a sentence using the word.

comfortable

_____

_____

_____

_____

Write in Response to Reading

Read page 28 from "Starting Out." Write your opinion on how well the illustration helps readers see the trees and lumberjacks from Paul's point of view. Support your writing using text evidence.

_____

_____

_____

_____

_____

Students demonstrate contextual understanding of Benchmark Vocabulary. Students read text closely and use text evidence in their written answers.

Name _____

Contributions of Illustrations to a Text

DIRECTIONS Using evidence from the text, answer the following questions about pages 28–31 of *Paul Bunyan*.

1. Look at the illustration on page 28. How does it help you understand why Babe can help Paul by pulling trees into stacks?

_____

_____

_____

2. Look at the illustration on page 29. What does it help you better understand about the Elmers?

_____

_____

_____

3. Look at the illustration on page 29. What does it help you better understand about the way the Elmers cut down trees?

_____

_____

_____

4. Look at the illustrations on pages 30 and 31. What do the illustrations help you understand about the environment in the dining hall?

_____

_____

_____

Students analyze and respond to literary and informational text.

Name _____

Gather Information from Print and Digital Sources Gather information from print and digital sources about the two pets you chose, and write down your opinion about which pet you think is the best to own. Then make a list of your sources.

_____

_____

_____

_____

_____

Conventions

Form Possessives

DIRECTIONS For each sentence, fill in the blank with the correct possessive form of the noun.

1. Babe was _____ (Paul) ox.

2. The cookhouse _____ (boys) roller skates helped them move quickly.

3. My class agreed with _____ (Charles) opinion about the story *Paul Bunyan*.

Students write routinely for a range of tasks, purposes, and audiences. Students practice various conventions of standard English.

Benchmark Vocabulary

Name _____

DIRECTIONS Write a sentence using the word.

huddled

_____

_____

_____

Read pages 32–35. Write an explanatory response about how the exaggerations help convey the central message. Use evidence from the text.

_____

_____

_____

_____

_____

_____

Students demonstrate contextual understanding of Benchmark Vocabulary. Students read text closely and use text evidence in their written answers.

Name _____

Taking Shelter

The first week of May in Tornado Alley was active that year. Nearly every day after school, Kirsten heard the tornado siren from the nearby Oklahoma town. She rushed to her basement for shelter.

Kirsten's friend Julia had never spent tornado season in the area. She was staying with Kirsten because her parents were out of town. As the girls talked in the yard, the tornado siren wailed. Kirsten bolted toward her house. Julia asked Kirsten what she was doing. "Going to the basement!"

Julia stared at Kirsten as if she were crazy and foolish. She said that she and her parents never did anything when they heard a siren. Just then, Kirsten saw her mom frantically waving from the porch. "Come in, girls!"

In the basement, Kirsten told her mom what Julia had said. Kirsten's mom looked at Julia. "Let me tell you just how important tornado sirens are. This house is not the same one we bought. A tornado smashed the first one."

Julia's heart raced. Kirsten's mom explained, "That tornado had winds of up to 165 miles per hour. It was given an EF-3 rating on the Fujita (foo-JEE-ta) Scale. Do you know what the Fujita Scale is?" Julia nodded.

Kirsten's mom described the sound that the tornado made. "It was like a freight train speeding by," she said. Julia turned pale. She missed her parents and promised Kirsten's mom that she and her parents would take her advice. They would take shelter when the siren sounded.

Students read text closely to determine what the text says.

Lesson 13

Name _____

Gather Evidence What traits would you use to describe each character in the story? Underline examples from the text to support your choices.

_____

_____

Gather Evidence: Extend Your Ideas Look at the traits you used to describe each character in the story. Make up a character and write 3–4 sentences describing him or her.

_____

_____

_____

Ask Questions Write two questions you would ask a tornado expert. Underline twice details in the text that support your questions.

_____

_____

Ask Questions: Extend Your Ideas Do you have questions about tornadoes that aren't answered in the text? Where could you find their answers?

_____

Make Your Case What do you think was the most convincing information that was shared with Julia to get her to promise to take cover next time? Circle it in the text, and write a sentence explaining your choice on a separate sheet of paper.

_____

Make Your Case: Extend Your Ideas On a separate piece of paper, write a persuasive paragraph about a topic you introduce to a character. What convincing information did you include?

Students read text closely to determine what the text says.

Name _____

Take Brief Notes on Sources Use your own words to take notes on the sources you found in Lesson 12. Your notes should describe facts and details that support your opinion (on which animal makes a better pet), as well as your reasons for this opinion. Organize your notes into categories. Write your notes on the lines below or on a separate sheet of paper.

_____

_____

_____

_____

_____

_____

Use Possessives

DIRECTIONS Make the sentences easier to follow by using a possessive noun to show ownership.

1. The shovels of the lumberjacks were worn down from shoveling

snow. _____

_____

2. The tunnels dug by the lumberjacks were deep under the snow.

_____

_____

3. The flames of the fire did not feel warm. _____

_____

Students write routinely for a range of tasks, purposes, and audiences. Students practice various conventions of standard English.

Name _____

DIRECTIONS Write a sentence using each word.

eager   groove   boulders

_____

_____

_____

_____

Write in Response to Reading

Read the description of how the Grand Canyon was formed on page 39. Write an interview with Paul Bunyan that gives his explanation of the process for creating the canyon and how he felt about it. Use details from the text in your interview.

_____

_____

_____

_____

_____

_____

Students demonstrate contextual understanding of Benchmark Vocabulary. Students read text closely and use text evidence in their written answers.

Name _____

Determine the Central Message

DIRECTIONS Using evidence from the text, answer the following questions about pages 38–41 from *Paul Bunyan*.

1. How was the Mississippi River created?

   _____

   _____

2. What caused Paul to accidentally create the Grand Canyon?

   _____

   _____

3. Why was Paul careful not to leave any footprints when he and Babe went out West?

   _____

   _____

   _____

4. What is the central message of the story? How do these events help develop the story's central message?

   _____

   _____

   _____

   _____

   _____

   _____

Students analyze and respond to literary and informational text.

Name _____

Plan and Prewrite Form an opinion about whether Paul is likeable, and think of reasons for your opinion. Take notes on details from the story that support your reasons. Then, on a separate sheet of paper, use this information to create an outline for an opinion essay.

_____

_____

_____

_____

_____

Conventions

Conventional Spelling for Suffixes

DIRECTIONS Read pages 38–41 of *Paul Bunyan*. Then list words from those pages that include the types of suffixes identified below.

1. List two words with a suffix that describes a past action.

_____

_____

2. List two adjectives with a suffix that turns it into an adverb.

_____

3. List two words with a suffix that describes an action that is happening now.

_____   _____

Students write routinely for a range of tasks, purposes, and audiences. Students practice various conventions of standard English.

Name _____

DIRECTIONS Write a sentence using each word.

stubborn   eager

_____

_____

_____

_____

Write in Response to Reading

Read "Growing Up" and "Moving On" in *Paul Bunyan*. Do you think Paul would have chosen to be a regular-sized person if he had had a choice? Support your response with evidence from the text.

_____

_____

_____

_____

_____

_____

Students demonstrate contextual understanding of Benchmark Vocabulary. Students read text closely and use text evidence in their written answers.

Name _____

Draft an Opinion Essay Use the outline you wrote in Lesson 14 to write a draft of your opinion essay. Your essay should include your opinion, reasons for that opinion, and evidence from the text that supports your reasons. Write your draft on a separate sheet of paper.

Conventions

Adjust Spellings for Endings

DIRECTIONS Read each sentence carefully. On the line next to the sentence, write *correct* if the underlined word is spelled correctly. If it is not, write the correct spelling on the line.

1. That winter was the <u>coldest</u> yet. _____

2. Paul's tennis shoes are <u>weter</u> than Amy's boots. _____

3. When Paul was a baby, his <u>crys</u> broke the windows. _____

Students write routinely for a range of tasks, purposes, and audiences. Students practice various conventions of standard English.

Name _____

Suffixes -er, -or, -ess, -ist

DIRECTIONS Add the suffix to each base word. Write the new word on the line.

1. edit + -or = _____

4. sell + -er = _____

2. art + -ist = _____

5. lion + -ess = _____

3. conduct + -or = _____

DIRECTIONS Write the word from the Word Bank that best fits each definition.

Word Bank

shipper	governess	biologist	diarist	investigator

_____ **6.** a person who keeps a diary

_____ **7.** one who ships packages

_____ **8.** one who investigates

_____ **9.** a scientist in the field of biology

_____ **10.** in past centuries, a woman who taught children

DIRECTIONS Add the suffix *-er, -or, -ess,* or *-ist* to the base word in parentheses to complete each sentence. Write the word on the line.

_____ **11.** Gertrude Ederle was the first woman (swim) to successfully cross the English Channel.

_____ **12.** Before the crossing, she had been a gold (medal) in the 1924 Olympics.

_____ **13.** She was quite a (competition), and held 29 U.S. and world records.

_____ **14.** Unlike Olympic skater Sonja Henie, Ederle did not become an (act).

_____ **15.** Instead, Ederle had a career as a swimming (instruct) for children with hearing difficulties.

Students apply grade-level phonics and word analysis skills.

Name _____

DIRECTIONS Write a sentence using each word.

ashamed   huddled

_____
_____
_____
_____

Write in Response to Reading

Read page 38 in *Paul Bunyan*. Do you believe the explanations for how the
Rocky Mountains and Mississippi River were created? Then read pages
18–28 in *Storm in the Night*. Do you believe Grandfather's story? Explain
why you do or do not believe the events from each story using evidence
from the texts.

_____
_____
_____
_____
_____

Students demonstrate contextual
understanding of Benchmark Vocabulary.
Students read text closely and use text
evidence in their written answers.

Name _____

Revise a Draft Revise the opinion essay you drafted in Lesson 15. Look for ways to use a more interesting word, avoid repeating the same words or phrases, add linking words and phrases, add or clarify details to explain reasons, and add or strengthen the concluding statement. Write your revised essay on a separate sheet of paper.

Conventional Spelling for High-Frequency Words

DIRECTIONS For each word, write *correct* if the word is spelled correctly or *incorrect* if the word is spelled incorrectly. Then write a sentence with the word, using its correct spelling.

1. thaught _____

_____

2. becawse _____

_____

3. favorite _____

_____

Students write routinely for a range of tasks, purposes, and audiences. Students practice various conventions of standard English.

Name _____

Benchmark Vocabulary

DIRECTIONS Write a sentence using each word.

> banished   secure   ecstatic   managed

_____

_____

_____

_____

_____

Write in Response to Reading

What central message do "The Myth of Icarus" and "Anansi's Long, Thin Legs: An African Fable" share? How is this message developed in both texts? Use evidence from both texts in your response. Write your answer below or on a separate sheet of paper.

_____

_____

_____

_____

_____

Students demonstrate contextual
understanding of Benchmark Vocabulary.
Students read text closely and use text
evidence in their written answers.

Name _____

Edit an Essay On a separate sheet of paper, edit the opinion essay you developed in Lessons 14–16. Correct any errors in grammar, capitalization, spelling, and punctuation. Then make sure that your essay has all of its parts.

Conventions

Consult a Dictionary to Check and Correct Spellings

DIRECTIONS Use a print or digital dictionary to check the spelling of each word below. If the word is spelled correctly, write *correct* on the line next to the word. If the word is spelled incorrectly, write the correct spelling on the line next to the word.

1. desparate _____

2. consert _____

3. triumphant _____

Students write routinely for a range of tasks, purposes, and audiences. Students practice various conventions of standard English.

Benchmark Vocabulary

Name _____

DIRECTIONS Write a sentence using each word.

hitched   comfortable   surround   mutterings

_____

_____

_____

_____

_____

Write in Response to Reading

Read page 40 in *Paul Bunyan*, page 20 in *Knots on a Counting Rope*, and page 30 in *Storm in the Night*. On a separate sheet of paper, write a brief essay in which you describe how each text conveys its central message or lesson through key details. Use evidence from the text in your response.

_____

_____

_____

_____

_____

_____

_____

Students demonstrate contextual understanding of Benchmark Vocabulary. Students read text closely and use text evidence in their written answers.

Name _____

Compare and Contrast

DIRECTIONS Using evidence from the texts, answer the following questions about *Knots on a Counting Rope*, *Storm in the Night*, and *Paul Bunyan*.

1. Which word or phrase could be used to describe the main characters in all three stories?

   _____

   _____

2. How does this trait help each main character? Explain your answer using details from the stories.

   _____

   _____

   _____

   _____

3. After reading all three stories, what might readers learn about the importance of having this trait?

   _____

   _____

   _____

4. From reading all three stories, what do readers learn about the purpose of telling stories?

   _____

   _____

   _____

Students analyze and respond to literary and informational text.

Name _____

Publish and Present Neatly write the final version of your opinion essay on a separate sheet of paper.

Capitalize Appropriate Words in Titles

DIRECTIONS Below are new titles for *Knots on a Counting Rope*, *Storm in the Night*, and *Paul Bunyan*. Rewrite the titles with correct capitalization.

1. the blue horses _____

2. thomas, grandfather, and the big storm _____

   _____

3. the strongest lumberjack in the world _____

   _____

Students write routinely for a range of tasks, purposes, and audiences. Students practice various conventions of standard English.

Name _____

Syllable Pattern VCCCV

DIRECTIONS Choose the word in parentheses with the VCCCV syllable pattern to finish each sentence. Write the word on the line.

_____ **1.** The (students/children) took a trip to the zoo.

_____ **2.** Their teachers arranged for a (surprise/selection).

_____ **3.** The zookeeper gave an (alert/address) to the group.

_____ **4.** She told them to (watch/inspect) each animal habitat.

_____ **5.** She said to (compare/contrast) the animals' homes.

_____ **6.** That day, they saw (dozens/hundreds) of animals.

DIRECTIONS Circle the word that has the VCCCV syllable pattern. Then write a sentence on the line that uses the word you circled.

7. forgive monster wonder

_____

8. human fortress winner

_____

9. complain number writer

_____

10. constant planet signal

_____

11. beyond robin sample

_____

12. chosen control copper

_____

Students apply grade-level phonics and word analysis skills.

Name _____

DIRECTIONS Write a sentence using each word.

atmosphere   extends   intense   equator   exchange

_____

_____

_____

_____

_____

_____

Write in Response to Reading

Read page 6 of *Weather.* Write a paragraph in which you discuss the relationship between insolation and the greenhouse effect, using text evidence to support your writing.

_____

_____

_____

_____

_____

_____

Students demonstrate contextual understanding of Benchmark Vocabulary. Students read text closely and use text evidence in their written answers.

Name _____

Convey Ideas and Information Think about the different types of weather you experience in your area during each season. Using a Four-Column Chart, with each of the seasons listed as headings, write down words that describe each season. Then think about whether today is a typical day for the season and whether it matches any of the words in your chart. Below, write a few sentences about today's weather and whether today is a seasonal day.

_____

_____

_____

_____

_____

_____

Conventions

Functions of Adverbs in Sentences

DIRECTIONS Circle the adverb in each sentence. Then write the word that the adverb modifies and whether it is a verb, an adjective, or another adverb.

1. A remarkably large thundercloud appeared in the distance.

   _____

2. The soft breeze blew gently through the trees. _____

3. Our journey began unusually early in the morning.

   _____

Students write routinely for a range of tasks, purposes, and audiences. Students practice various conventions of standard English.

Name _____

DIRECTIONS Write a sentence using each word.

rotation   currents   altitude   continuous   advances

_____

_____

_____

_____

_____

_____

_____

Write in Response to Reading

Read the first sentence on page 10 of *Weather*. Write an opinion paragraph stating whether or not you agree that weather-related issues are not simple. Use text evidence to support your writing.

_____

_____

_____

_____

_____

Students demonstrate contextual understanding of Benchmark Vocabulary. Students read text closely and use text evidence in their written answers.

Name _____

Scientific Ideas

DIRECTIONS Using evidence from the text, answer the following questions about pages 10–15 from *Weather*.

1. What effect does the difference in the speeds of rotation at Earth's equator and near the poles have on winds and ocean currents?

_____

_____

_____

_____

2. How much of the sun's energy is absorbed by forests and trees? How much of the sun's energy is reflected by a fresh snowfall?

_____

_____

_____

3. What is a *front?* What is the difference between a cold front and a warm front?

_____

_____

_____

_____

Students analyze and respond to literary and informational text.

Name _____

Understand and Identify Genre Choose a U.S. city to research. Use the weather site your teacher assigned to research today's weather and tomorrow's forecast for your chosen city. Take notes on your research. Then identify the genre of informative writing that you would produce from these notes, and briefly explain why you chose this genre.

_____

_____

_____

_____

_____

_____

Conventions

Review of Adverbs in Sentences

DIRECTIONS Underline the adverb in each sentence. Then write the verb the adverb modifies and whether the adverb describes *how, when,* or *where* the action takes place.

1. We left town yesterday around noon. _____

2. I dashed upstairs to grab my umbrella. _____

3. She threw her books carelessly on the table. _____

Students write routinely for a range of tasks, purposes, and audiences. Students practice various conventions of standard English.

Name _____

DIRECTIONS Write a sentence using each word.

properties   unstable   unsettled

_____

_____

_____

_____

Write in Response to Reading

Read pages 16–21 of *Weather*. Select one type of cloud, and write a paragraph about it. Use text evidence to support your writing.

_____

_____

_____

_____

_____

Students demonstrate contextual understanding of Benchmark Vocabulary. Students read text closely and use text evidence in their written answers.

Lesson 3

Name _____

Weather Work

Do you need a jacket today? Will you need an umbrella? Meteorologists help us answer those kinds of weather questions. Meteorologists are more than just the people on TV telling us what the weather is going to be like today. Meteorologists are scientists. They go to school to learn all about the weather and what creates it.

Predicting the weather is a big part of being a meteorologist. Today, meteorologists depend on technology and weather observers around the world to help them.

Weather observers are very important to meteorologists. These observers make measurements every day at nearly 10,000 different weather stations. Thousands of ships at sea record the weather also. More than 500 weather stations release weather balloons. The balloons collect weather data. All of this data is closely examined. Then the data is used to make weather predictions.

Being a meteorologist is an important job! Meteorologists help us stay safe during dangerous weather. They work with city managers to plan the number of snowplows needed during winter storms. They provide information to power companies. This helps the companies meet energy needs during hot or cold spells. They even help sporting event organizers predict whether a game can go on after a rain delay.

The next time you watch a meteorologist on TV, keep in mind that the two-minute weather forecast is based on hours of research. Three cheers for meteorologists!

Students read text closely to determine what the text says.

Name _____

Gather Evidence Circle the clues in "Weather Work" that tell you the writer's opinion about meteorologists.

Gather Evidence: Extend Your Ideas Do you agree or disagree with the writer? Write three sentences stating your opinion using text evidence.

_____

_____

_____

Ask Questions Underline information from the text that you have questions about.

Ask Questions: Extend Your Ideas Write down two questions you have about meteorologists after reading "Weather Work."

_____

_____

Make Your Case How did the writer group information in the selection? Draw a box around one or two words or phrases that you think best describe the information in each paragraph.

Make Your Case: Extend Your Ideas Look at the words you boxed. Underline twice supporting details you found in the paragraphs.

Students read text closely to determine what the text says.

Choose Details Use key details to determine the main idea of pages 16–21 of *Weather*. Then use examples to show how the main idea is supported in the text. Write a paragraph explaining how the author used key details to support the main idea of the text to inform readers about the topic.

_____

_____

_____

_____

_____

_____

Conventions

Use of Comparative Adverbs

DIRECTIONS Read each sentence and look at the adverb in parentheses. Rewrite the sentence to include the comparative form of the adverb.

1. The clouds moved (fast) across the sky than they did before.

_____

_____

2. The sun rose a little (early) today than it did yesterday.

_____

_____

3. The rain came down (gently) than it did this morning.

_____

_____

Students write routinely for a range of tasks, purposes, and audiences. Students practice various conventions of standard English.

Name _____

DIRECTIONS Write a sentence using each word.

condensed   resistance   evaporates

_____

_____

_____

_____

Write in Response to Reading

Skim pages 22–27 of *Weather*, and then write an opinion paragraph about the photographs on those pages. Do the photographs add to the text? Are different photographs needed? Support your writing by using text evidence.

_____

_____

_____

_____

_____

_____

Students demonstrate contextual understanding of Benchmark Vocabulary. Students read text closely and use text evidence in their written answers.

Name _____

Information from Illustrations

DIRECTIONS Using evidence from the text, answer the following
questions about pages 22–27 from *Weather*.

1. How do the text on page 22 and the photograph on page 23 work
   together to help the reader understand the concept of precipitation?

   _____

   _____

   _____

2. How do the photographs on page 24 support the text information on
   this page?

   _____

   _____

   _____

3. What does the photograph on page 25 show? What information does
   this image provide that is not provided in the text?

   _____

   _____

   _____

4. What text detail about frost does the photograph on page 27
   illustrate?

   _____

   _____

   _____

Students analyze and respond to literary and
informational text.

Name _____

Introduce the Topic Choose a weather-related topic, and use a Main Idea graphic organizer to plan the main idea and key details you will write about. Below, write the sentences that will introduce the topic, including a sentence that will grab the reader's interest and attention.

_____

_____

_____

_____

_____

Conventions

Use Superlative Adverbs

DIRECTIONS Complete each sentence with the superlative form of the verb in parentheses.

1. My two friends and I ran home to escape the hail, and I ran _____ (far).

2. A brief rainstorm has hit the area each day for the past three days, but today's rainstorm hit _____ (hard).

3. Of all the weather predictions the meteorologist has made this week, she predicted today's weather _____ (accurately).

Students write routinely for a range of tasks, purposes, and audiences. Students practice various conventions of standard English.

Name _____

DIRECTIONS Write a sentence using each word.

conditions   reduce   irritate

_____

_____

_____

_____

Write in Response to Reading

Read the first two paragraphs on page 30 of *Weather*. Write a paragraph that explains the scientific ideas that lead to the creation of smog pollution, using text evidence to support your writing.

_____

_____

_____

_____

_____

🏠 Students demonstrate contextual understanding of Benchmark Vocabulary. Students read text closely and use text evidence in their written answers.

Lesson 5

Name _____

Writing

Develop a Topic Use the graphic organizer you created in Lesson 4 to develop your topic with facts, definitions, and details for an informational news report. Identify facts, definitions, and details to develop your topic, and then write a news report that is one or two paragraphs long. Use the lines below or a separate sheet of paper.

_____

_____

_____

_____

_____

Conventions

Select Comparative or Superlative Adverbs

DIRECTIONS Circle the comparative or superlative adverb that correctly completes each sentence.

1. Today it's snowing much (harder / hardest) than it was last week.

2. Of all the local teens who shovel snow, Janine shovels the (more carefully / most carefully).

3. The blizzard arrived much (earlier / earliest) than the meteorologist predicted.

Students write routinely for a range of tasks, purposes, and audiences. Students practice various conventions of standard English.

Name _____

Syllable Pattern CV/VC

DIRECTIONS Circle the word with two vowels together where each vowel has a separate vowel sound. Then draw a line between the letters that stand for the separate sounds.

1. clean   plain   radios

2. audience   faith   search

3. either   medium   southern

4. beach   pound   pioneer

5. greed   journal   ideas

6. reality   poison   waiter

7. stadium   grain   group

8. freeze   create   stream

DIRECTIONS Read the paragraph. Words with two vowels together are underlined. Circle the underlined words in which the two vowels have separate sounds. The vowels may or may not be followed by a consonant. Write the words on the lines.

<u>Maria</u> wants to know the <u>reasons</u> for different musical <u>sounds</u>. Her mother is a <u>violinist</u> and her father is a <u>pianist</u>. Both instruments have strings that can be plucked or hit. <u>Would</u> a plucked <u>violin</u> string <u>sound</u> like a hit <u>piano</u> string? To find <u>out</u>, she <u>created</u> a <u>duet</u> for her parents. They played it in a <u>giant</u> recording <u>studio</u>. The results <u>influenced</u> <u>Maria's</u> <u>scientific</u> study of music.

9. _____   13. _____   17. _____

10. _____   14. _____   18. _____

11. _____   15. _____   19. _____

12. _____   16. _____   20. _____

Students apply grade-level phonics and word analysis skills.

Name _____

DIRECTIONS Write a sentence using each word.

atmosphere   intense   absorbed

_____

_____

_____

_____

Write in Response to Reading

Look at the photograph on page 31 of *Weather*. Describe the photograph. How is the picture related to the text? Does it help you better understand the text? Why or why not?

_____

_____

_____

_____

_____

Students demonstrate contextual understanding of Benchmark Vocabulary. Students read text closely and use text evidence in their written answers.

Name _____

Group Related Information Group related information for the topic of your news report, organize the information into categories using a Web B graphic organizer, and use this information in your news report.

_____

_____

_____

_____

_____

_____

Conventions

Select Comparative or Superlative Adverbs

DIRECTIONS Read the sentences in items 1–3. Combine the sentences in each item into an original sentence using the comparative or superlative form of the adverb in parentheses. Write the new sentence on the line.

1. The ice in the sun melts. The ice in the shade melts. (fast)

_____

_____

2. Earth rotates at the equator. Earth rotates at the poles. (rapidly)

_____

_____

3. I skied one mile. She skied two miles. He skied three miles. (far)

_____

_____

Students write routinely for a range of tasks, purposes, and audiences. Students practice various conventions of standard English.

Name _____

DIRECTIONS Write a sentence using each word.

properties   unstable   unsettled

_____

_____

_____

_____

Write in Response to Reading

Read page 18 of *Weather*. Write a paragraph that explains the difference between literal and nonliteral uses of words and phrases, using text evidence to support your writing.

_____

_____

_____

_____

_____

Students demonstrate contextual understanding of Benchmark Vocabulary. Students read text closely and use text evidence in their written answers.

Lesson 7

Language Analysis

Name _____

Literal and Nonliteral Meanings

DIRECTIONS Using evidence from the text, answer the following questions about *Weather*.

1. Read the first sentence of the second paragraph on page 4. Explain the nonliteral meaning of the word *ocean* in this sentence. Then state its literal meaning.

   _____

   _____

   _____

2. In the second paragraph on page 10, the author uses the word *colorful* to describe the names of regional winds. What are the literal and nonliteral meanings of *colorful*?

   _____

   _____

3. Read the third paragraph on page 16. Does the word *families* in the first sentence have a literal or nonliteral meaning? Explain.

   _____

   _____

   _____

4. Read the first paragraph on page 30. Is the meaning of the word *troubled* in the last sentence literal or nonliteral? Explain.

   _____

   _____

   _____

Students analyze and respond to literary and informational text.

Name _____

Use Illustrations Create an illustration for your news report. The illustration should provide additional facts, definitions, or details that support the main idea of your news report. You may need to include a caption or a label to help readers understand the main idea and details of the illustration. Use the space below to write notes about your illustration.

_____

_____

_____

_____

_____

_____

Conventions

Define Abstract Nouns

DIRECTIONS Circle the abstract noun in each sentence. Then write whether each noun names a feeling or a quality.

1. Curiosity is important if you want to become a scientist.

   _____

2. The meteorologist's dedication to her work was admirable.

   _____

3. I shared his delight at the news that the rain would stop by midday.

   _____

Students write routinely for a range of tasks, purposes, and audiences. Students practice various conventions of standard English.

Benchmark Vocabulary

Name _____

DIRECTIONS Write a sentence using each word.

hoist   axis   orbits   humid

_____

_____

_____

_____

_____

Write in Response to Reading

Read page 54 in the *Text Collection*. The words *wide* and *dry* are used to describe a plain in the text. These words can be used to describe many things in real life, such as a classroom board (wide) and unused paper towels (dry). What else can you use these words to describe? Support your answers with evidence from the text.

_____

_____

_____

_____

_____

_____

Students demonstrate contextual
understanding of Benchmark Vocabulary.
Students read text closely and use text
evidence in their written answers.

Name _____

Connect Ideas Within Categories Add linking words and phrases to your news report. Identify linking words and phrases that connect similar ideas and those that connect contrasting ideas. Then use them to connect events in your news report. Write your revised report on the lines below or on a separate sheet of paper.

_____

_____

_____

_____

_____

Use Abstract Nouns

DIRECTIONS Circle the abstract noun in each sentence. On the line, write an original sentence that contains the abstract noun you circled.

1. The beauty of the winter landscape inspired me to take a photograph.

_____

2. Her determination to pursue a career as a meteorologist was inspiring.

_____

3. He showed great courage when navigating the ship through rough waters.

_____

Students write routinely for a range of tasks, purposes, and audiences. Students practice various conventions of standard English.

Name _____

DIRECTIONS Write a sentence using each word.

hoist   axis

_____

_____

_____

_____

Write in Response to Reading

Read pages 56–57 of the *Text Collection*. Write a paragraph stating your opinion about how the author describes weather and its causes around the world. Use evidence from the text to support your answers.

_____

_____

_____

_____

_____

_____

_____

Students demonstrate contextual understanding of Benchmark Vocabulary. Students read text closely and use text evidence in their written answers.

Name _____

Scientific Ideas

DIRECTIONS Using evidence from the text, answer the following questions about pages 45–56 of the *Text Collection*.

1. Read page 45. What happens to the snow fort in Alberta, Canada? What causes this event to happen?

   _____

   _____

2. Read page 52. What happens when the rains come to Northern Kenya? What effect does this have on the people's actions? What effect does the author suggest will happen when the sun shines?

   _____

   _____

   _____

   _____

3. Read the second paragraph on page 56. What happens to the North Pole and the South Pole in March? What effect does this have on the Arctic and Antarctica?

   _____

   _____

   _____

   _____

Students analyze and respond to literary and informational text.

Name _____

Provide a Concluding Statement Write a concluding statement for your news report. First, review your writing for details that support your main idea. Then ask yourself why you chose the topic or what you found the most interesting about it. Use this information to help you come up with a concluding statement that summarizes your report, gives the reader something to think about, or wraps up the information in an interesting way.

_____

_____

_____

_____

_____

Conventions

Form the Past Tense of Irregular Verbs

DIRECTIONS Circle the present-tense verb in each sentence. Then identify the correct past-tense form of the verb. On the line, rewrite the sentence with the past-tense verb.

1. I drive slowly and carefully through the snowstorm.

_____

2. Due to the falling temperature, the water freeze.

_____

3. Many difficulties arise because of the icy streets.

_____

Students write routinely for a range of tasks, purposes, and audiences. Students practice various conventions of standard English.

Name _____

DIRECTIONS Write a sentence using each word.

conditions   reduce   irritate   humid

_____

_____

_____

_____

_____

_____

Write in Response to Reading

Read page 50 of the *Text Collection* and page 16 of *Weather*. In your opinion, which text does a better job of expressing its key details? Use specific examples from the texts to support your answer.

_____

_____

_____

_____

_____

Students demonstrate contextual understanding of Benchmark Vocabulary. Students read text closely and use text evidence in their written answers.

Name _____

Provide a Concluding Section Review the writing work that you completed in Lessons 4–9. Create a concluding section for your news report on the lines below. Then write the final version of your news report on a separate sheet of paper.

_____

_____

_____

_____

_____

_____

Conventions

Use the Past Tense of Irregular Verbs

DIRECTIONS Circle the past-tense verb that correctly completes each sentence. Then use the past-tense verb in an original sentence. Write the new sentence on the line.

1. The storm (becomed / became) so severe that we stayed home.

_____

2. The lightning bolt hit the tree branch and (broke / breaked) it.

_____

3. They went outside and (maked / made) a snowman after the blizzard.

_____

Students write routinely for a range of tasks, purposes, and audiences. Students practice various conventions of standard English.

Name _____

Homophones

DIRECTIONS Choose the word that best matches each definition. Write the word on the line.

_____ **1.** a small room in a prison   sell   cell

_____ **2.** to record on paper   write   right

_____ **3.** 60 minutes   hour   our

_____ **4.** not strong   week   weak

_____ **5.** a period of darkness   night   knight

_____ **6.** swallowed   eight   ate

_____ **7.** a story   tail   tale

_____ **8.** also   to   too

DIRECTIONS Choose the word that best matches each definition. Write the word on the line.

_____ **9.** My aunt (cent/sent) us a text.

_____ **10.** We couldn't (hear/here) each other on the phone.

_____ **11.** Her text said she would (meet/meat) us outside.

_____ **12.** Our (plain/plane) arrived late, though.

_____ **13.** We looked everywhere and could not (sea/see) her.

_____ **14.** Finally, (eye/I) spotted her bright green van.

_____ **15.** Then I (new/knew) we would be fine.

Students apply grade-level phonics and word analysis skills.

Name _____

DIRECTIONS Write a sentence using each word.

predictable   damage   preparations   evacuate   devastated

_____

_____

_____

_____

_____

_____

_____

Read page 12 of *Living Through a Natural Disaster*. Write a paragraph to explain some measures the city of Darwin has taken to be prepared for another cyclone. Use evidence from the text to support your answer.

_____

_____

_____

_____

_____

Students demonstrate contextual
understanding of Benchmark Vocabulary.
Students read text closely and use text
evidence in their written answers.

Name _____

Recall Information from Experiences Complete the Web A graphic organizer to recall information about a significant weather event you have experienced in your lifetime. Then write the details in the space below.

_____

_____

_____

_____

_____

_____

Function of Past-Tense Verbs

DIRECTIONS Use the past-tense form of the verb in parentheses to complete each sentence.

1. During last night's storm, I _____ (accept) his offer of an umbrella.

2. She _____ (clean) the floor after the dog ran through the kitchen with muddy paws.

3. The floor got muddy because the dog _____ (disobey) his owner's command to "Stay."

Students write routinely for a range of tasks, purposes, and audiences. Students practice various conventions of standard English.

Name _____

DIRECTIONS Write a sentence using each word.

meanders   nourishes   erosion   irrigation

_____

_____

_____

_____

_____

Write in Response to Reading

Read page 20 of *Living Through a Natural Disaster.* Do you believe that people living near the Huang River are safer now than in years past? Use evidence from the text to support your answer.

_____

_____

_____

_____

_____

Students demonstrate contextual
understanding of Benchmark Vocabulary.
Students read text closely and use text
evidence in their written answers.

Use Illustrations

DIRECTIONS Using evidence from the text, answer the following questions about pages 13–20 of *Living Through a Natural Disaster.*

1. Look at the diagram on page 16. What is the main cause of the water rising in the river?

   _____

2. What should readers understand after viewing the diagram "How the Huang He Became So High"?

   _____

   _____

   _____

3. How are the details in the text on pages 16–17 different from the information in the diagram?

   _____

   _____

   _____

4. Look at the photo on page 20 of the Huang He today. How do the photo and key details from the text help readers understand how the Huang He has changed in some areas?

   _____

   _____

   _____

Students analyze and respond to literary and informational text.

Name _____

Take Brief Notes and Quote from a Text Write a paragraph that answers a research question about the Huang He flood, using your notes from the text.

_____

_____

_____

_____

_____

_____

Conventions

Function of Irregular Past-Tense Verbs

DIRECTIONS Circle the past-tense verb in each sentence. On the short line, write whether the circled past-tense verb is regular or irregular. Then use the circled verb in an original sentence. Write the new sentence on the long line.

1. I listened to the weather forecast this morning. _____

_____

2. The family swam in the ocean during the trip. _____

_____

3. They built a dike to keep the river from overflowing. _____

_____

Students write routinely for a range of tasks, purposes, and audiences. Students practice various conventions of standard English.

Name _____

DIRECTIONS Write a sentence using each word.

affects   diverse   habitats   consequences   international

_____

_____

_____

_____

_____

_____

_____

Write in Response to Reading

Read page 28 of *Living Through a Natural Disaster.* What are some ways the El Niño of 1997 has helped people plan and prepare for future disasters? Use evidence from the text in your answer.

_____

_____

_____

_____

_____

Students demonstrate contextual understanding of Benchmark Vocabulary. Students read text closely and use text evidence in their written answers.

Name _____

Be Prepared!

Are you ready for an emergency? In school, you prepare with practice drills in case of a fire, tornado, or hurricane. Do you practice being ready for an emergency at home?

You need to put together an emergency kit! This kit should always be kept in a place at home that is easy to remember and find. If disaster hits, the emergency kit should supply you with everything you need. You should be prepared to be without electricity or water for a couple of days.

One of the most important supplies in an emergency kit is water. You'll need one gallon of water per person in your family for at least three days. You should also have three days' worth of food. Food needs to be nonperishable. That means food that cannot spoil. Foods like granola bars, canned tuna, dried fruits, and crackers are some examples.

A radio that can be powered by batteries is also important. You'll need to know what is happening. Be sure to have extra batteries in your emergency supply kit too. Flashlights, a whistle to signal for help, and a first-aid kit are also very important.

Once you create your emergency supply kit, be sure to check your food and water supplies every six months. You may want to replace them then to have fresh food and water on hand.

During an emergency, always remember to remain calm. Knowing that you have planned ahead and are prepared can be very reassuring.

Students read text closely to determine what the text says.

Gather Evidence Circle clues in the text that tell you how important the writer thinks emergency supply kits are.

Gather Evidence: Extend Your Ideas Do you agree with the writer? If you do, explain why. If you do not, research emergency supply kits and provide 2–3 more reasons why emergency supply kits are important.

_____

_____

Ask Questions Underline phrases or sentences in the text that you have questions about.

Ask Questions: Extend Your Ideas Write two questions you would ask a disaster volunteer about preparing for an emergency.

_____

_____

Make Your Case How did the writer organize information in the selection? What other way do you think it could have been arranged? Explain your thinking. Draw a box around important phrases or sentences in the selection.

_____

_____

_____

_____

Make Your Case: Extend Your Ideas On a separate piece of paper, write an example paragraph of another way the selection could have been arranged. Include the important phrases you drew a box around.

Students read text closely to determine what the text says.

Name _____

Sort Evidence from Notes On a separate sheet of paper, complete a Three-Column Chart graphic organizer to sort information from *Living Through a Natural Disaster* into categories. You can use this graphic organizer to compare two of the disasters, using the third column for categories. You can also compare three disasters using one or two categories or compare details under three subtopics for a single category.

Form Irregular Past-Tense Verbs

DIRECTIONS Read each sentence. Then rewrite the sentence using the past-tense form of the underlined verb.

1. Hurricanes <u>bring</u> floods to Honduras and Nicaragua.

_____

2. The people <u>know</u> that El Niño <u>is</u> strong.

_____

3. Many areas <u>are</u> affected by El Niño.

_____

Students write routinely for a range of tasks, purposes, and audiences. Students practice various conventions of standard English.

Name _____

DIRECTIONS Write a sentence using each word.

organizations   traumatized   monitor   invaluable

_____

_____

_____

_____

_____

Read page 29 of *Living Through a Natural Disaster.* Is it important for people to learn from past natural disasters? Use evidence from the text in your answer.

_____

_____

_____

_____

_____

Students demonstrate contextual understanding of Benchmark Vocabulary. Students read text closely and use text evidence in their written answers.

Name _____

Plan and Prewrite an Informational Essay Write an outline of an informational essay that will explain how climate has impacted your daily life in some way.

_____

_____

_____

_____

_____

_____

Form Simple Verb Tenses

DIRECTIONS Read each sentence. Then rewrite the sentence using the form of the underlined verb that is shown in parentheses.

1. Meteorologists study data about Earth's atmosphere. (past tense)

_____

2. Natural disasters affect huge groups of people. (future tense)

_____

3. Disaster-relief agencies helped many people. (present tense)

_____

Students write routinely for a range of tasks, purposes, and audiences. Students practice various conventions of standard English.

Name _____

DIRECTIONS Write a sentence using each word.

damage   preparations   evacuate

_____

_____

_____

_____

Write in Response to Reading

Read page 5 of *Living Through a Natural Disaster,* and write a paragraph giving the name and a brief description of each type of disaster outlined in the text. Support your writing with evidence from the text.

_____

_____

_____

_____

_____

_____

Students demonstrate contextual understanding of Benchmark Vocabulary. Students read text closely and use text evidence in their written answers.

Name _____

Scientific Ideas

DIRECTIONS Using evidence from the text, answer the following questions about *Living Through a Natural Disaster.*

1. Why was Cyclone Tracy so destructive?

   _____

   _____

   _____

   _____

2. How does human activity cause floods?

   _____

   _____

   _____

   _____

3. What makes the plains near the Huang He in China so fertile?

   _____

   _____

4. What caused the Huang He flood of 1933?

   _____

   _____

   _____

   _____

Students analyze and respond to literary and informational text.

Name _____

Draft an Informational Essay On a separate sheet of paper, write a draft of an informational essay that will explain how climate has impacted your daily life in some way.

Form and Use Simple Verb Tenses

DIRECTIONS Complete each sentence with the present, past, or future tense of the verb in parentheses. The verb must make sense in the sentence.

1. Extreme rainfall can _____ many problems for people who live near rivers. (cause)

2. Hurry, the eye of the cyclone _____ soon! (pass)

3. Last year's drought _____ the land. (dry)

Students write routinely for a range of tasks, purposes, and audiences. Students practice various conventions of standard English.

Name _____

Vowel Patterns *a, au, aw, al, augh, ough*

DIRECTIONS Choose the word with the vowel sound in **ball.** Write the word on the line.

_____ **1.** The (cause/meaning) of our move was to be near family.

_____ **2.** Now we live in a (tiny/small) apartment.

_____ **3.** I really miss having a (lawn/yard) to run around on.

_____ **4.** Sometimes we (speak/talk) about our old home.

_____ **5.** The ocean and the (palm/oak) trees were wonderful.

_____ **6.** We often (found/caught) fish and ate them for dinner.

_____ **7.** We (usually/always) agree that we are glad we moved.

_____ **8.** That is because we (wanted/thought) of our family.

DIRECTIONS Write *a, au, aw, al, augh,* or *ough* to complete each word. Write the whole word on the line.

_____ **9.** I picture my grandmother wrapped in her purple sh___l.

_____ **10.** I remember the scent of her delicious tomato s___ce.

_____ **11.** I miss the s___sage she cooked for our dinner.

_____ **12.** Sometimes it was so spicy, it made me c___!

_____ **13.** But grandmother t___t us to enjoy what we have now.

_____ **14.** We can w___k to our cousins' houses whenever we want.

_____ **15.** We can also c_ll grandmother to tell her we miss her.

Students apply grade-level phonics and word analysis skills.

Name _____

DIRECTIONS Write a sentence using each word.

condensed   resistance   evaporates   affects   diverse   habitats

_____

_____

_____

_____

_____

_____

_____

Write in Response to Reading

Revisit the photographs in *Weather* and *Living Through a Natural Disaster*. In your opinion, are the captions that describe the events happening in the photographs necessary? Use specific examples from the texts to support your answer.

_____

_____

_____

_____

_____

Students demonstrate contextual understanding of Benchmark Vocabulary. Students read text closely and use text evidence in their written answers.

Name _____

Contribution of Maps, Photographs, and Illustrations

DIRECTIONS Using evidence from the texts, answer the following questions about *Weather* and *Living Through a Natural Disaster*.

1. What does the diagram on page 8 of *Weather* show? How does it support the information on page 9?

   _____

   _____

   _____

2. What does the diagram on page 8 of *Living Through a Natural Disaster* show? How does it support the information on page 8?

   _____

   _____

   _____

3. Think about these two diagrams and other diagrams in both texts. How are the authors' use of diagrams in *Weather* and *Living Through a Natural Disaster* similar?

   _____

   _____

4. How are the authors' use of maps in *Weather* and *Living Through a Natural Disaster* similar?

   _____

   _____

5. How are the authors' use of maps in *Weather* and *Living Through a Natural Disaster* different?

   _____

   _____

Students analyze and respond to literary and informational text.

Name _____

Revise an Informational Essay On a separate sheet of paper, revise the draft of your informational essay that explains how climate has impacted your daily life.

Form Simple Sentences

DIRECTIONS Use information from *Weather* and *Living Through a Natural Disaster* and the directions below to write simple sentences.

1. Write a simple sentence with a singular subject and a verb that is in the present tense.

_____

2. Write a simple sentence with a plural subject and a verb that is in the past tense.

_____

3. Write a simple sentence with a singular subject and a verb that is in the past tense.

_____

Students write routinely for a range of tasks, purposes, and audiences. Students practice various conventions of standard English.

Name _____

DIRECTIONS Write a sentence using each word.

orbits   nourishes   erosion   irrigation

_____

_____

_____

_____

_____

Write in Response to Reading

Explain how the authors of *On the Same Day in March* and *Living Through a Natural Disaster* use key details to support a main idea. Use specific examples from the texts to support your answer.

_____

_____

_____

_____

_____

Students demonstrate contextual understanding of Benchmark Vocabulary. Students read text closely and use text evidence in their written answers.

Name _____

Edit a Piece of Writing On a separate sheet of paper, edit your paragraphs that explain how climate has impacted your daily life in some way. Examine your essay with a focus on word choice and sentence structure. Have you chosen the best words to say what you mean? Have you used varied sentence structure to give your writing a better flow? Keep these questions in mind as you edit your work.

Conventions

Form Compound Sentences

DIRECTIONS Choose the conjunction *and, but, yet, or,* or *so* to correctly complete the following compound sentences about *On the Same Day in March* and *Living Through a Natural Disaster.*

1. I thought spring would never come, _____ finally the March chinook is here!

2. In central Thailand in March, it is too hot to plant rice, _____ it is too hot to pick rice.

3. Floods from the Huang He used to be a big problem, _____ today parts of the river are nearly dry.

Students write routinely for a range of tasks, purposes, and audiences. Students practice various conventions of standard English.

Name _____

DIRECTIONS Write a sentence using each word.

altitude   continuous   advances   axis   traumatized   monitor   invaluable

_____

_____

_____

_____

_____

_____

Write in Response to Reading

Locate related events, concepts, or processes in *On the Same Day in March*, *Weather*, and *Living Through a Natural Disaster*. In your opinion, which author does the best job of expressing the relationships between those events, concepts, or processes? Use specific examples from the texts to support your answer.

_____

_____

_____

_____

_____

Students demonstrate contextual understanding of Benchmark Vocabulary. Students read text closely and use text evidence in their written answers.

Name _____

Publish and Present Think of unusual ideas for presenting your work. For example, after you have published your essay, work with the whole class or in a smaller group to coordinate the presentation of your work. Have the assigned timekeeper, recorder, and manager work together to make sure everyone participates and stays on task. Write your ideas for presenting your work on the lines below. Finally, present your essay.

_____

_____

_____

_____

_____

Conventions

Form Complex Sentences

DIRECTIONS Create a complex sentence using each pair of sentences.

1. The drought in Central America worsened. Costa Rica still did not ask for aid. _____

_____

2. The Kenyan people hurried to play in the river. It would soon dry up.

_____

_____

3. Trees absorb most of the sun's energy that falls on them. A fresh snowfall reflects most of the sun's energy. _____

_____

_____

Students write routinely for a range of tasks, purposes, and audiences. Students practice various conventions of standard English.

Name _____

Vowel Patterns *ei, eigh*

DIRECTIONS Read each sentence. Underline the word that has *ei* or *eigh*. Write *long a, long e,* or *long i* on the line to tell what sound the vowel pattern stands for.

_____ 1. We enjoy shopping at our neighborhood bakery.

_____ 2. We always go on either Friday or Saturday.

_____ 3. Shelves of baked goods reach from floor to ceiling.

_____ 4. I'm not the right height to reach the top shelf.

_____ 5. That shelf must be eight feet high!

_____ 6. We weigh all our choices and make up our minds.

_____ 7. At last, we receive our package from the baker.

DIRECTIONS Choose a word from the Word Bank to match each clue. Write the word on the line. You will use each word just once.

Word Bank

deceive	freight	height	leisure
neighbor	rein	seize	vein

_____ 8. a strap used to control a horse

_____ 9. to grab an object

_____ 10. free time

_____ 11. a person who lives nearby

_____ 12. the distance up from the ground

_____ 13. cargo a truck carries from one place to another

_____ 14. not tell the truth

_____ 15. a blood vessel in a living creature's body

Students apply grade-level phonics and word analysis skills.

Name _____

DIRECTIONS Write a sentence using each word.

scratchy   fierce   belong   pale   punchy

_____

_____

_____

_____

_____

_____

_____

Write in Response to Reading

Write a paragraph about the boy in the story. Describe what he is like, what he does, and how he feels. Remember to use text evidence to support your ideas.

_____

_____

_____

_____

_____

_____

Students demonstrate contextual understanding of Benchmark Vocabulary. Students read text closely and use text evidence in their written answers.

Name _____

Write About Genre: Historical Fiction Write a paragraph in which you explain what is fiction and what is fact in the historical fiction *Back of the Bus*. Support your opinion with reasons and evidence from the text.

_____

_____

_____

_____

_____

Conventions

Identify Nouns

DIRECTIONS Read these sentences from *Back of the Bus*. Underline the nouns. Then circle the noun that serves as a subject in the sentence. Tell whether each noun names a person, place, animal, or thing.

1. Mama shakes "no" at me, and I hold it snug in my hand.

_____

2. That breeze is long gone, and I want me a drink real bad.

_____

3. That policeman clicks them metal things on her hands, quick and loud like the screen door slammin', and off the bus they go.

_____

Name _____

DIRECTIONS Write a sentence using each word.

scratchy   fierce   belong   pale   punchy

_____

_____

_____

_____

_____

_____

_____

Write in Response to Reading

Read *Back of the Bus*. Write a paragraph in which you state an opinion about whether Mama and the other passengers should have defended Rosa. Support your opinion with text evidence.

_____

_____

_____

_____

_____

Students demonstrate contextual understanding of Benchmark Vocabulary. Students read text closely and use text evidence in their written answers.

Name _____

Write About Theme Write a paragraph that tells the central message of *Back of the Bus*. Use examples from the text to support your choice.

_____

_____

_____

_____

_____

_____

Conventions

Form Regular Plural Nouns

DIRECTIONS Read page 66 of *Back of the Bus*. Choose three singular nouns from the page. Add endings to them to make them plural, and write the plural noun on the line. Then write a sentence with the plural noun.

1. _____

_____

2. _____

_____

3. _____

_____

Students write routinely for a range of tasks, purposes, and audiences. Students practice various conventions of standard English.

Benchmark Vocabulary

Name _____

DIRECTIONS Write a sentence using each word.

aisle   jammed   growly   hush

_____

_____

_____

_____

_____

Write in Response to Reading

Read *Back of the Bus*. Write a paragraph in which you state an opinion about what Mama thinks about what Rosa Parks does. Support your opinion with text evidence.

_____

_____

_____

_____

_____

_____

Students demonstrate contextual understanding of Benchmark Vocabulary. Students read text closely and use text evidence in their written answers.

Name _____

Real-Life Connections Between Words and Their Use

DIRECTIONS Using evidence from the text, answer the following questions about *Back of the Bus*.

1. Find the word *fierce* on page 74. Use the word *fierce* to tell about something in your life.

_____

_____

2. Now use the word *fierce* to tell about something in the world.

_____

_____

3. Find the word *clicks* on page 77. Use the word *clicks* to tell about something in your life that makes the same noise.

_____

_____

4. Now use the word *clicks* to tell about something in the world.

_____

_____

5. Find the phrase "pale and punchy" on page 78. The author uses this phrase to explain that the boy feels dazed. Use the phrase "pale and punchy" to describe something in your life.

_____

_____

Students analyze and respond to literary
and informational text.

Name _____

Don't Give Up!

What do Sonia Sotomayor, Walt Disney, Dr. Seuss, and Thomas Edison have in common? They have become famous, successful people—but they didn't start out that way!

Sonia Sotomayor has overcome many challenges. She grew up poor and lost her father when she was young. She spoke only Spanish as a child. However, she studied hard in school and became a lawyer. Today she serves on the United States Supreme Court. She is only the third woman to do so.

Walt Disney was fired from his newspaper job and told he had a poor imagination. Today, Disney's ideas inspire theme parks and a movie company.

Theodor Geisel, also known as Dr. Seuss, wrote his first book called *And to Think That I Saw It on Mulberry Street*. After many different book companies turned it down, one company printed it. He went on to write over 40 children's books.

These people might have just given up, but they *didn't*. They kept trying and became successful.

Thomas Edison didn't give up, either. He invented many things, including a long-lasting light bulb. It took him hundreds of tries before he found the materials that worked best for this invention. He never thought of himself as a failure. He said, "I have not failed. I've just found ten thousand ways that won't work."

Every time Edison tried something that didn't work, he got one step closer to finding a way that *would* work.

So the next time you're trying to learn something new or solve a problem, don't stop trying. You may be just one step away from success!

Students read text closely to determine what the text says.

Name _____

Gather Evidence Box phrases and sentences in the article that explain how the author feels about failure.

Gather Evidence: Extend Your Ideas Did you box "These people might have just given up, but they didn't. They kept trying and became successful"? How are the clues you boxed good signs the author feels strongly about not giving up? Write one or two sentences explaining how.

_____

_____

Ask Questions Underline two facts about one of the people in this article. Write a question that can be answered by the facts you chose.

_____

_____

Ask Questions: Extend Your Ideas If you could talk to one of the famous people mentioned in this article, with whom would you talk and what would you ask? Make a list of the questions you would like to ask.

_____

_____

Make Your Case Circle what you think is the most important reason the writer gives to support the conclusion to this selection. Explain your choice below.

_____

_____

Make Your Case: Extend Your Ideas On a separate sheet of paper, write a paragraph that tells another way the conclusion to the selection could have been reached. Make sure to use the important reason you circled.

Students read text closely to determine what the text says.

Name _____

Author's Purpose and Forming Opinions Pretend you are going to interview Rosa Parks about taking action and making changes. On a separate sheet of paper, write ten interview questions that you would ask Rosa Parks. Then write one sentence stating an opinion about Rosa Parks's impact on the United States.

Form Irregular Plural Nouns

DIRECTIONS Complete each sentence below with the plural form of the noun in parentheses.

1. I watched my older brother build _____ (shelf) for his room.

2. There were five _____ (man) in the car.

3. Sarah watched the _____ (goose) swim across the pond.

Students write routinely for a range of tasks, purposes, and audiences. Students practice various conventions of standard English.

Benchmark Vocabulary

Name _____

DIRECTIONS Write a sentence using each word.

bravery   dignity

_____

_____

_____

_____

Write in Response to Reading

Read *Back of the Bus* and *Rosa Parks: Hero of Our Time*. Using information from both texts, write a paragraph in which you explain what Rosa Parks did and how it changed things for all Americans.

_____

_____

_____

_____

_____

_____

Students demonstrate contextual understanding of Benchmark Vocabulary. Students read text closely and use text evidence in their written answers.

Name _____

Compare and Contrast

DIRECTIONS Using evidence from the texts, answer the following questions about *Rosa Parks*: *Hero of Our Time* and *Back of the Bus*.

1. How do both *Back of the Bus* and *Rosa Parks: Hero of Our Time* show the effect Rosa Parks's actions have on other African Americans?

_____

_____

_____

_____

_____

_____

_____

2. At the end of *Rosa Parks: Hero of Our Time*, the author writes, "Rosa Parks's bravery helped make life better for all Americans." How is this idea shown in *Back of the Bus?*

_____

_____

_____

_____

_____

_____

Students analyze and respond to literary and informational text.

Name _____

State an Opinion State an opinion that responds to the following prompt: *What makes a good citizen?* First, complete the following sentence frames:

1. The most important thing a good citizen does is _____.

2. An important character trait for a good citizen to have is _____.

Then use your responses to develop your opinion statement, and write it on the lines below. Remember that you should support your opinion with reasons.

_____

_____

_____

_____

_____

_____

Conventions

Use Irregular Plural Nouns

DIRECTIONS Create a sentence using the plural form of each noun.

1. child _____

_____

2. deer _____

_____

3. life _____

_____

Students write routinely for a range of tasks, purposes, and audiences. Students practice various conventions of standard English.

Name _____

DIRECTIONS Write a sentence using each word.

immigrants   hire   filthy   fined   fired   inspected

_____

_____

_____

_____

_____

_____

_____

Write in Response to Reading

Read pages 8–11 from *Brave Girl*. Write a paragraph describing Clara's job based on information in the text and the illustrations.

_____

_____

_____

_____

_____

_____

Students demonstrate contextual understanding of Benchmark Vocabulary. Students read text closely and use text evidence in their written answers.

Name _____

Introduce the Topic Write a few sentences that introduce the topic for your opinion piece about what makes a good citizen. Think about your opinion statement from Lesson 4 as you write your introduction.

_____

_____

_____

_____

_____

_____

Conventions

Suffixes and Base Words

DIRECTIONS Add the suffix *-ness, -er, -less,* or *-y* to each base word from the text. Write the new word and a definition on the line.

1. dirt _____

2. tall _____

3. move _____

4. job _____

Students write routinely for a range of tasks, purposes, and audiences. Students practice various conventions of standard English.

Name _____

Suffixes *-y, -ish, -hood, -ment*

DIRECTIONS Combine the base word and the suffix. Write the new word on the line.

1. pay + -ment = _____

2. cloud + -y = _____

3. self + -ish = _____

4. child + -hood = _____

5. storm + -y = _____

6. excite + -ment = _____

7. false + -hood = _____

8. baby + -ish = _____

DIRECTIONS Add *-y, -ish, -hood,* or *-ment* to the base word in parentheses to best complete each sentence. Write the new word on the line.

_____ 9. During my (child), we moved often.

_____ 10. We live in one (neighbor) with woods and a pond.

_____ 11. Playing outdoors provided lots of (entertain).

_____ 12. One (snow) day, we decided to go skating on the pond.

_____ 13. A (move) at the edge of the pond frightened us.

_____ 14. How (fool) we felt when we saw it was our neighbor.

_____ 15. Soon we were all skating in the (frost) air.

Students apply grade-level phonics and word analysis skills.

Name _____

DIRECTIONS Write a sentence using each word.

     imagined   union   punished   pickets   arrest

_____

_____

_____

_____

_____

_____

_____

Write in Response to Reading

Read pages 15–17 from *Brave Girl*. Write a paragraph telling why Clara wants the factory girls to strike and what she hopes they will gain from a strike.

_____

_____

_____

_____

_____

_____

Students demonstrate contextual understanding of Benchmark Vocabulary. Students read text closely and use text evidence in their written answers.

Name _____

Provide Reasons to Support an Opinion Write sentences stating three reasons that support your opinion about what makes a good citizen.

_____

_____

_____

_____

_____

_____

Prefixes and Base Words

DIRECTIONS Add the prefix *dis-, un-, over-,* or *under-* to the base words. Write the new word and a definition on the line.

1. afraid _____

2. do _____

3. fed _____

4. pay _____

Students write routinely for a range of tasks, purposes, and audiences. Students practice various conventions of standard English.

Name _____

DIRECTIONS Write a sentence using each word.

speech   meeting   proposes   patience   revolt   bravest

_____

_____

_____

_____

_____

_____

_____

Write in Response to Reading

Read pages 21–23 from *Brave Girl*. What do you think about Clara's actions at the union meeting? Write a paragraph that states your opinion and supports it with reasons and evidence from the text.

_____

_____

_____

_____

_____

Students demonstrate contextual
understanding of Benchmark Vocabulary.
Students read text closely and use text
evidence in their written answers.

Name _____

Point of View

DIRECTIONS Using evidence from the text, answer the following questions about page 28 from *Brave Girl*.

1. Read page 28. What is the author's point of view about bringing about change in America?

   _____

   _____

   _____

2. What details from the text reveal the author's point of view?

   _____

   _____

   _____

   _____

   _____

   _____

   _____

3. What is your point of view about bringing about change in America?

   _____

   _____

   _____

Students analyze and respond to literary and informational text.

Name _____

Create an Organizational Structure On a separate sheet of paper, write several paragraphs that answer the following prompt: *What makes a good citizen?* After writing the introduction you created in Lesson 5, organize your reasons from Lesson 6, and write one paragraph for each reason.

Conventions

Define Abstract Nouns

DIRECTIONS Underline the abstract noun(s) in each sentence from *Brave Girl*.

1. Throngs of workers pack the seats, the aisles, the walls—the hall thrums with excitement.

2. Her singing lifts the spirits of the picketers.

3. They shorten the workweek and raise salaries.

Students write routinely for a range of tasks, purposes, and audiences. Students practice various conventions of standard English.

Name _____

DIRECTIONS Write a sentence using each word.

industry   abuses   affluent   publicize   negotiate   hazardous

_____

_____

_____

_____

_____

_____

_____

Write in Response to Reading

Read page 31 from *Brave Girl*. What were the effects of the 1909 strike?
Use evidence from the text to support your answer.

_____

_____

_____

_____

_____

_____

_____

Students demonstrate contextual
understanding of Benchmark Vocabulary.
Students read text closely and use text
evidence in their written answers.

Name _____

Using Linking Words and Phrases On a separate sheet of paper, revise your paragraphs from Lesson 7 by adding linking words and phrases to link your opinion to your reasons.

Conventions

Abstract Nouns

DIRECTIONS Underline the abstract noun in each sentence. Then write whether the abstract noun is a subject, direct object, or an object of a preposition in the sentence.

1. Many wrongs still exist in this country. _____

2. Clara had a lot of courage. _____

3. He felt joy when he saw his new bicycle. _____

Students write routinely for a range of tasks, purposes, and audiences. Students practice various conventions of standard English.

Name _____

DIRECTIONS Write a sentence using each word.

immigrants   arrest   proposes   negotiate

_____

_____

_____

_____

_____

_____

Write in Response to Reading

Do you think Clara Lemlich is a good subject for a biography? Why or why not? State your opinion and give reasons to support it.

_____

_____

_____

_____

_____

_____

Students demonstrate contextual understanding of Benchmark Vocabulary. Students read text closely and use text evidence in their written answers.

Name _____

Provide Concluding Statement and Outline Concluding Section Write a concluding statement, and outline a concluding section about how Clara Lemlich and Rosa Parks are active citizens.

_____

_____

_____

_____

_____

_____

Conventions

Define Pronouns

DIRECTIONS Underline the pronoun(s) in each pair of sentences below. Then tell what noun it replaces, whether the pronoun is singular or plural, and whether it is a subject, object, or possessive pronoun.

1. Clara marched for workers' rights. She did not give up.

_____

2. The factory owners did not like Clara. She made trouble for them.

_____

3. Clara was a hero. Her bravery inspired other workers.

_____

Students write routinely for a range of tasks, purposes, and audiences. Students practice various conventions of standard English.

Name _____

DIRECTIONS Write a sentence using each word.

jammed   growly   hire   meeting   industry

_____
_____
_____
_____
_____
_____
_____

Write in Response to Reading

What important point do both *Back of the Bus* and *Brave Girl* make? How does each text develop this point? Use evidence from both texts to support your answer.

_____
_____
_____
_____
_____
_____

Students demonstrate contextual understanding of Benchmark Vocabulary. Students read text closely and use text evidence in their written answers.

Name _____

Compare and Contrast

DIRECTIONS Using evidence from the texts, answer the following questions about *Back of the Bus* and *Brave Girl*.

1. How are Rosa Parks and Clara Lemlich similar?

   _____

   _____

2. How are the actions that Rosa Parks and Clara Lemlich took different?

   _____

   _____

   _____

3. Which groups did Rosa Parks and Clara Lemlich help?

   _____

   _____

4. What are the similarities between the groups of people Rosa Parks and Clara Lemlich helped?

   _____

   _____

   _____

Students analyze and respond to literary and informational text.

Name _____

Provide a Concluding Section Write a concluding section based on the concluding statement and outline you created in Lesson 9. First, rewrite your concluding statement from Lesson 9. Then, using the outline you created, write at least two more sentences that you can use with your concluding statement to make a concluding section.

_____

_____

_____

_____

_____

_____

Use Pronouns

DIRECTIONS On the lines below, write two sentences about the events in *Back of the Bus* and one sentence about the events in *Brave Girl* that include pronouns. Underline the pronouns you use in each sentence.

1. _____

_____

2. _____

_____

3. _____

_____

Students write routinely for a range of tasks, purposes, and audiences. Students practice various conventions of standard English.

Name _____

Vowel Digraphs *oo, ew, ue, ui*

DIRECTIONS Circle each word with the vowel sound in **moon** or the vowel sound in **foot**. Then write each word in the correct column.

1. The entire school spent a day at the art center in our neighborhood.

2. It took the whole day to see all of the famous paintings and statues.

3. We looked at works by some of the art world's true masters.

4. The next day, our teacher had us make new drawings in our notebooks.

5. I drew President Lincoln wearing black wool clothing and a tall hat.

vowel sound in moon   **vowel sound in foot**

6. _____   11. _____

7. _____   12. _____

8. _____   13. _____

9. _____   14. _____

10. _____   15. _____

DIRECTIONS Cross out the one word in each line that does **not** have the vowel sound in **moon** or the vowel sound in **foot**.

16. build   soot   glue

17. hook   rocket   smooth

18. button   bookstore   juice

19. football   stew   story

20. dew   cook   throat

Students apply grade-level phonics and word analysis skills.

Name _____

DIRECTIONS Write a sentence using each word.

sly   freedom   resolve   clambered   spry   absent

_____

_____

_____

_____

_____

_____

Write in Response to Reading

Read the final two lines of "The Little Black-Eyed Rebel" on page 123. What do you think the black-eyed rebel is trying to say? Use evidence from the text to support your answer.

_____

_____

_____

_____

_____

Students demonstrate contextual understanding of Benchmark Vocabulary. Students read text closely and use text evidence in their written answers.

Name _____

Research: Gather Information Find at least two print or digital sources to support your opinion writing. Remember that you are responding to the following prompt: *What impact did Rosa Parks have on her community?* List your sources below, and explain why each one will be helpful.

_____

_____

_____

_____

_____

_____

Conventions

Function of Pronouns

DIRECTIONS Complete each sentence with an appropriate pronoun. Then, on the line next to the sentence, write down the noun it replaces.

1. The workers were so busy that _____ could not fix the potholes in the road. _____

2. Kim went to the store yesterday, and _____ bought some apples. _____

3. The students must practice in order to improve _____ writing skills. _____

Students write routinely for a range of tasks, purposes, and audiences. Students practice various conventions of standard English.

Name _____

DIRECTIONS Write a sentence using each word.

loyal   dare   race   justice   opportunity

_____

_____

_____

_____

_____

_____

_____

Write in Response to Reading

In your opinion, which author does the best job of conveying the central message of her poem? Use text evidence to support your answer.

_____

_____

_____

_____

_____

Students demonstrate contextual understanding of Benchmark Vocabulary. Students read text closely and use text evidence in their written answers.

Name _____

Determine the Central Message

DIRECTIONS Using evidence from the texts, answer the following questions about "Brother Against Brother," "Dare," and "Where?"

1. In "Brother Against Brother," what do the soldiers see when they look "into the enemy's eyes"? How do these details point to the central message of the poem?

_____

_____

_____

_____

2. What word is emphasized in "Dare"? How does this detail contribute to the central message of the poem?

_____

_____

_____

_____

3. Where are the "small places" mentioned in the poem "Where?" How does this detail add to the central message of the poem?

_____

_____

_____

_____

Students analyze and respond to literary and informational text.

Name _____

Research: Take Notes Pair up with a classmate. Take turns pretending to be Rosa Parks. Interview each other, using the ten interview questions you wrote in Lesson 3. On the lines below or on a separate sheet of paper, take notes on your partner's responses. Include direct quotations where appropriate. Then revise and rewrite your opinion from Lesson 3 about Rosa Parks's impact on the United States.

_____

_____

_____

_____

_____

Conventions

Function of Pronouns in Particular Sentences

DIRECTIONS Read each pair of sentences, and underline the pronoun in the second sentence. On the line below the sentences, tell which noun the pronoun replaces and whether it serves as a subject, object, or possessive.

1. Laura Purdie Salas is an author. She wrote "Dare."

_____

2. The book includes Eleanor Roosevelt's poem "Where?" Her poem expresses an opinion about human rights.

_____

3. I like poems. I can read them quickly.

_____

Students write routinely for a range of tasks, purposes, and audiences. Students practice various conventions of standard English.

Name _____

DIRECTIONS Write a sentence using each word.

Titanic   voyage   cramped   decks   longingly

_____

_____

_____

_____

_____

_____

_____

Write in Response to Reading

The word *amazing* is used on page 8 and page 12 of *Below Deck*:
A Titanic Story. Why do you think the author uses this word? Think of
some synonyms for the word *amazing*. If the author had used one of those
synonyms instead of *amazing*, would it have changed the meaning of the
sentences? Why or why not?

_____

_____

_____

_____

_____

Students demonstrate contextual
understanding of Benchmark Vocabulary.
Students read text closely and use text
evidence in their written answers.

Name _____

Honoring Code Talkers

On July 26, 2001, four Native Americans received the Congressional Gold Medal. It is the highest civilian award the U.S. Congress can give. These men were survivors of the Navajo Code Talkers. The Code Talkers used their native language to send secret messages during World War II. It took about 60 years for them to be recognized for their service.

Inside the Capitol in Washington, D.C., President George W. Bush addressed the audience. He said, "Today, America honors 21 Native Americans who, in a desperate hour, gave their country a service only they could give."

Bill Toledo was a Code Talker for three years. On the island of Guam, he barely missed being hit by sniper bullets. Thanks to his quick feet, he escaped unharmed. Later, while marching through the jungle, he was mistaken for a Japanese soldier. He was taken prisoner at gunpoint. The mistake was soon realized. He was given a bodyguard so it would not happen again. The Code Talkers were very important to the war effort.

Mr. Toledo said that it's important to share his experiences with younger generations. He wants them to understand that freedom comes at a cost. He wants them to appreciate the sacrifices that service people have made. It is these sacrifices that have helped Americans keep our freedom.

Students read text closely to determine what the text says.

Name _____

Gather Evidence Circle phrases and sentences in the article that tell how the author feels about the Code Talkers.

Gather Evidence: Extend Your Ideas Do you agree with the author? Explain why or why not in two or three sentences.

_____

_____

Ask Questions Underline two sentences in the selection that you have questions about. Using the Internet or an encyclopedia, research the questions and write the answers you find.

_____

_____

Ask Questions: Extend Your Ideas Write two factual questions and two opinion questions you would ask a Code Talker about his experience.

_____

_____

_____

Make Your Case What do you think is most important for a reader to know about World War II to better understand this selection? How does knowing about history help you better understand selections such as this one? Draw a box around a sentence in the article that you think you would understand better if you had more historical knowledge.

_____

_____

Make Your Case: Extend Your Ideas On a separate sheet of paper, work with a partner to write any historical information you can remember that would help answer your questions. Then research your questions using an encyclopedia or the Internet.

Students read text closely to determine what the text says.

Name _____

Sort Evidence into Categories Remember that you will be writing an essay that gives your opinion about Rosa Parks and how her actions helped her community. On the lines below or on a separate sheet of paper, sort into categories the evidence about Parks that you gathered from your sources in Lesson 11. After taking notes on the evidence you have gathered and sorted, determine the best way to organize the information, and create a final version of your organizer on a separate sheet of paper.

_____

_____

_____

_____

_____

_____

Conventions

Ensure Pronoun-Antecedent Agreement

DIRECTIONS Underline each pronoun and circle its antecedent. If the two agree, write *correct* on the line. If they do not agree, rewrite the sentence to correct the error in pronoun-antecedent agreement.

1. Grace put their suitcase under the bunk. _____

_____

2. The passengers danced and clapped her hands. _____

_____

3. The man was tall and handsome, and his clothes looked expensive.

_____

Students write routinely for a range of tasks, purposes, and audiences. Students practice various conventions of standard English.

Name _____

DIRECTIONS Write a sentence using each word.

stationary   abandon   chaos   panic

_____

_____

_____

_____

_____

Write in Response to Reading

Read pages 22–40 of *Below Deck*: A Titanic *Story*. Write a paragraph that explains how the events in the second half of the story build on the events in the first half.

_____

_____

_____

_____

_____

Students demonstrate contextual understanding of Benchmark Vocabulary. Students read text closely and use text evidence in their written answers.

Parts of Stories

DIRECTIONS Using evidence from the text, answer the following questions about pages 22–40 from *Below Deck: A Titanic Story*.

1. What two events does Grace remember when she has to decide whether or not to help Catherine? How do they affect her decision?

_____

_____

_____

_____

2. What happens after Grace gets Catherine and herself back to the main deck of the ship?

_____

_____

3. Why is Grace allowed onto the lifeboat?

_____

_____

4. Why do Catherine's parents say that they will take care of Grace?

_____

_____

Students analyze and respond to literary and informational text.

Name _____

Plan and Prewrite an Opinion Essay Create an outline for your opinion essay about Rosa Parks.

_____

_____

_____

_____

_____

_____

Conventions

Form Possessives

DIRECTIONS Complete each sentence with the possessive form of the noun in parentheses.

1. _____ (Grace) photo of Aunt Nora was in her suitcase.

2. The crewmen lowered the _____ (ship) lifeboats into the water.

3. Grace could hear the _____ (passengers) cries of terror.

Students write routinely for a range of tasks, purposes, and audiences. Students practice various conventions of standard English.

Name _____

DIRECTIONS Write a sentence using each word.

future   rooted   launched

_____

_____

_____

_____

Write in Response to Reading

What important decisions do Grace and Catherine make toward the end of the story? How do those decisions help develop the story's central message? Support your writing with text evidence.

_____

_____

_____

_____

_____

Students demonstrate contextual understanding of Benchmark Vocabulary. Students read text closely and use text evidence in their written answers.

Name _____

Draft an Opinion Essay On a separate sheet of paper, write a draft of your opinion essay about Rosa Parks and the impact of her actions on her community. Use the outline you created in Lesson 14 as a guide as you draft your essay.

Conventions

Using Possessives

DIRECTIONS Rewrite each sentence to use the possessive form of the underlined noun.

1. The lights of the <u>ship</u> went out.

   _____

2. The seats of the <u>lifeboat</u> were almost full.

   _____

3. The crewman would have kept Grace from entering the lifeboat if the parents of <u>Catherine</u> had not spoken up.

   _____

   _____

Lesson 16

Name _____

Phonics

Schwa

DIRECTIONS Choose the word with a vowel that has the same sound as the underlined vowels in **about, tak<u>e</u>n, penc<u>i</u>l, lem<u>o</u>n,** and **circ<u>u</u>s** to complete each sentence. Write the word on the line.

_____ **1.** Kim was too (afraid/lazy) to walk the dog.

_____ **2.** If Kim opened the door, the (rascal/dog) would run off.

_____ **3.** Kim usually took the dog to a (nearby/local) dog park.

_____ **4.** All the (animals/pets) were fetching and running.

_____ **5.** Kim could let the dog run (freely/happily) there.

_____ **6.** Kim kept dog treats in a (paper/plastic) bag.

_____ **7.** The dog (hurried/ran) back for a treat.

_____ **8.** In fact, the dog was always (ready/eager) for a treat.

DIRECTIONS Circle the letter in each word that stands for the same sound as the underlined vowels in **about, tak<u>e</u>n, penc<u>i</u>l, lem<u>o</u>n,** and **circ<u>u</u>s**.

9. kitchen   **12.** family   **15.** level   **18.** ago

10. river   **13.** melon   **16.** dollar   **19.** open

11. surprise   **14.** sugar   **17.** bushel   **20.** canyon

Students apply grade-level phonics and word analysis skills.

Name _____

DIRECTIONS Write a sentence using each word.

imagined patience hazardous decks longingly abandon

_____

_____

_____

_____

_____

_____

Write in Response to Reading

Recall the main events in *Brave Girl* and *Below Deck: A* Titanic *Story*.
How are Clara's and Grace's actions similar and different? Use text
evidence in your response.

_____

_____

_____

_____

_____

_____

Students demonstrate contextual
understanding of Benchmark Vocabulary.
Students read text closely and use text
evidence in their written answers.

Name _____

Revise a Draft On a separate sheet of paper, revise the opinion essay you drafted in Lesson 15. As you revise your essay, keep in mind that your essay should address the following question: *What impact did Rosa Parks have on her community?* Add linking words and phrases to connect your ideas. Add details or make them clearer to better explain your reasons, and make sure your evidence supports your opinion.

Use Commas in Dialogue

DIRECTIONS Add commas to correctly punctuate the dialogue.

1. "I want to go to school " said Clara.

2. "This ship is very large " said Grace. "I suppose I must board it now."

3. Clara said "We should go on strike!"

Students write routinely for a range of tasks, purposes, and audiences. Students practice various conventions of standard English.

Name _____

DIRECTIONS Write a sentence using each word.

fierce   punchy   bravest   longingly

_____

_____

_____

_____

_____

Write in Response to Reading

In your opinion, which author does the best job of describing characters and their roles in the events of the text? Use specific examples from the texts to support your answer.

_____

_____

_____

_____

_____

_____

Students demonstrate contextual understanding of Benchmark Vocabulary. Students read text closely and use text evidence in their written answers.

Name _____

Compare and Contrast

DIRECTIONS Using evidence from the texts, answer the following questions about *Brave Girl*, *Back of the Bus*, and *Below Deck*: *A Titanic Story*.

1. How are the actions of Rosa Parks, Clara Lemlich, and Grace similar?

   _____

   _____

   _____

2. How are the effects of their actions similar?

   _____

   _____

   _____

3. How are the consequences of Rosa Parks's and Clara Lemlich's actions similar?

   _____

   _____

   _____

4. How are the consequences of Grace's and Clara Lemlich's actions different from those of Rosa Parks's actions?

   _____

   _____

   _____

Students analyze and respond to literary and informational text.

Lesson 17

Name _____

Writing

Edit an Opinion Piece Read the revised version of your opinion essay closely, and correct any errors you find. Look for errors in grammar, capitalization, punctuation, and spelling. On a separate sheet of paper, write the edited version of your opinion essay.

Conventions

Use Quotation Marks in Dialogue

DIRECTIONS Add quotation marks to correctly punctuate the dialogue.

1. I'm going to miss you, Auntie Nora,   said Grace.   I love you so much.

2. Clara cried,   We must hold a general strike!

3. What is that policeman doing here, Mama?   I asked.

Students write routinely for a range of tasks, purposes, and audiences. Students practice various conventions of standard English.

Unit 4 • Module A • Lesson 17 • 355

Name _____

DIRECTIONS Write a sentence using each word.

burrows   release   beams   harbor   plunked

_____

_____

_____

_____

_____

_____

_____

Write in Response to Reading

How does each scene in *Rescue the Pufflings!* build on the scene before it to convey the central message of the play? Use evidence from the text to support your answer.

_____

_____

_____

_____

_____

_____

Students demonstrate contextual understanding of Benchmark Vocabulary. Students read text closely and use text evidence in their written answers.

Publish and Present Opinion Essays On a separate sheet of paper, write a final copy of your opinion essay that is free of errors. Then publish and present your essay by creating an audio or audio and video recording.

Using Commas in Addresses

DIRECTIONS Add commas to correctly punctuate the sentence and addresses.

1. The children went with their parents to Houston Texas to visit their grandmother.

2. John and Jane Williams
   987 Washington Avenue
   Tucson Arizona 63774

3. Laura and Keith Bridges
   134 Main Street
   Columbus Ohio 43085

Students write routinely for a range of tasks, purposes, and audiences. Students practice various conventions of standard English.

Name _____

Schwa

DIRECTIONS Circle the unaccented syllable or syllables in each word.

1. flavor   4. occur   7. level

2. arrange   5. merrily   8. gargle

3. version   6. cocoon   9. passenger

DIRECTIONS Choose the word with a vowel that has the same sound as the underlined vowels in **about, taken, pencil, lemon,** and **circus.** Write the word on the line.

_____	**10.** believe	cannon	feeling
_____	**11.** below	pancake	bustle
_____	**12.** compare	daily	remark
_____	**13.** branched	resume	welcome
_____	**14.** swallow	likable	heavy
_____	**15.** predict	summarize	review
_____	**16.** mixture	oatmeal	fancy
_____	**17.** seashore	reckless	decision
_____	**18.** award	airport	attic
_____	**19.** audio	visible	massive
_____	**20.** tender	orange	festive

Students apply grade-level phonics and word analysis skills.

Name _____

DIRECTIONS Write a sentence using each word.

system   goods   export

_____

_____

_____

_____

Write a paragraph that explains what you think the second duty of government should be. Use evidence from the text to support your answer.

_____

_____

_____

_____

_____

_____

Students demonstrate contextual understanding of Benchmark Vocabulary. Students read text closely and use text evidence in their written answers.

Name _____

Main Idea and Details

DIRECTIONS Using evidence from the text, answer the following questions about pages 4–9 from *What Is a Government?*

1. What is the main idea of the section "What Do Governments Do?"

   _____

   _____

2. Why is the money system important in a government?

   _____

   _____

3. Which details support the main idea that all children have a right to an education?

   _____

   _____

4. Which details help explain the importance of passing laws?

   _____

   _____

5. Which details explain how a national government protects its country?

   _____

   _____

Students analyze and respond to literary and informational text.

Name _____

Express a Point of View Read pages 4–9 of *What Is a Government*?
Write one sentence that expresses your own point of view about something
you read and one sentence that expresses an opposing point of view.

_____

_____

_____

_____

_____

Conventions

Subject-Verb Agreement

DIRECTIONS Circle the form of the verb that agrees in number with
the subject.

1. Governments (make/makes) laws.

2. A school (educate/educates) children.

3. They always (vote/votes) on election day.

Students write routinely for a range of tasks,
purposes, and audiences. Students practice
various conventions of standard English.

Name _____

DIRECTIONS Write a sentence using each word.

expectations   inspired   exception   influential   ruthlessness

_____

_____

_____

_____

_____

_____

_____

Write in Response to Reading

Read the paragraph about Sulayman I on page 14 and Elizabeth I on page 15. These rulers governed wisely but many other rulers did not. Do you think a wise ruler or a democracy is the best government? Support your ideas by using text evidence.

_____

_____

_____

_____

_____

Students demonstrate contextual understanding of Benchmark Vocabulary. Students read text closely and use text evidence in their written answers.

Name _____

Text Features and Search Tools

DIRECTIONS Using evidence from the text, answer the following questions about pages 10–15 from *What Is a Government?*

1. How do the photographs and their captions on pages 10–11 help you understand how the development of governments changed communities?

   _____

   _____

   _____

   _____

2. Look at the photographs and illustrations on pages 14–15. Which image is different from the others? What important idea does it help emphasize?

   _____

   _____

   _____

3. Read the captions of the photographs and illustrations on pages 14–15. Which caption gives information not provided in the others? What is the information?

   _____

   _____

   _____

   _____

Students analyze and respond to literary and informational text.

Lesson 2

Name _____

Understand Genres Write a few sentences about an opinion genre you have recently read. Explain how you knew you were reading an opinion genre. Then state your opinion about the genre, including whether you liked reading it, how strong you thought the author's reasons were, and whether you agreed or disagreed with the author's opinion.

_____

_____

_____

_____

_____

Ensure Subject-Verb Agreement

DIRECTIONS Complete each sentence with the correct present-tense form of the verb in parentheses.

1. John _____ (carry) his backpack to class.

2. The sailor _____ (row) the boat.

3. The student _____ (watch) the clock.

Students write routinely for a range of tasks, purposes, and audiences. Students practice various conventions of standard English.

Benchmark Vocabulary

Name _____

DIRECTIONS Write a sentence using each word.

representatives   consulted   intervene

_____

_____

_____

_____

Write in Response to Reading

Write a paragraph to explain the author's point of view about democracies.
Support your ideas by using text evidence.

_____

_____

_____

_____

_____

_____

Students demonstrate contextual
understanding of Benchmark Vocabulary.
Students read text closely and use text
evidence in their written answers.

The Election

It was time for the school elections. Each class was supposed to vote on who would represent it in the school congress. A committee was formed of third, fourth, and fifth graders. Its job was to choose the best voting process. Everyone had ideas about how the voting should be done.

Anton, a fifth grader, thought everyone should fill out a ballot. The voting station would be in the school cafeteria. At lunch, each student would write a candidate's name on a piece of paper and put it into a box. Then the votes would be counted.

Nisha, a fourth grader, thought that each class should vote for a representative. Then each grade would vote for those winners to select a representative for each grade.

Scotty, a third grader, thought that each grade should have an assembly to choose its representative. Someone would call out a candidate's name. Then students would raise their hands if they wanted that person to represent them. The person who got the most hands raised would be the winner.

The students went round and round about what they should do. Finally, they asked a teacher for her thoughts. "We're having a hard time agreeing on the voting process for the election," they said to the teacher.

"Why not vote on it?" asked Mrs. Hanson.

Students read text closely to determine what the text says.

Name _____

Gather Evidence The election committee had several ideas for the voting process. Circle similarities between the voting suggestions.

Gather Evidence: Extend Your Ideas Write two sentences about the differences between the voting processes. Why do you think each student chose his or her method of voting?

_____

_____

Ask Questions When the committee asked the teacher for help, what questions might she have asked the committee to help it reach a decision? Circle the question she asked the committee in the selection, and then write two questions she might have asked.

_____

_____

Ask Questions: Extend Your Ideas Why do you think the teacher resolved the situation the way she did? Write two to three sentences explaining her reasoning.

_____

_____

Make Your Case Circle an opinion held by one of the students. Give one reason that explains why that method of voting would work well.

_____

_____

Make Your Case: Extend Your Ideas Give one reason that explains why that method of voting would *not* work well.

_____

_____

Students read text closely to determine what the text says.

Name _____

Write About Reading Write one paragraph expressing an opinion about something you read on pages 16–21 in *What Is a Government?* Focus on one of the types of government described on those pages, and then express an opinion about the reading. Remember that you can write an opinion about the book's subject matter, organization, or illustrations, among other things.

_____

_____

_____

_____

_____

Conventions

Subject-Verb Agreement

DIRECTIONS In each sentence, underline the phrase or clause that comes between the subject and the verb. Then write whether the subject is singular or plural on the line, and circle the correct verb to complete the sentence.

1. The governments of many countries (is / are) democratic. _____

2. The U.S. president, who is elected by citizens, (serve / serves) a term of four years. _____

3. Most members of the Canadian parliament (belong / belongs) to political parties. _____

Students write routinely for a range of tasks, purposes, and audiences. Students practice various conventions of standard English.

Lesson 4

Benchmark Vocabulary

Name _____

DIRECTIONS Write a sentence using each word.

candidates   opposition   colonies

_____

_____

_____

_____

Write in Response to Reading

Write a paragraph to state your opinion about age requirements for voting.
Support your ideas by using text evidence.

_____

_____

_____

_____

_____

_____

Students demonstrate contextual
understanding of Benchmark Vocabulary.
Students read text closely and use text
evidence in their written answers.

Name _____

Literal and Nonliteral Meanings

DIRECTIONS Using evidence from the text, answer the following questions about pages 23–25 from *What Is a Government?*

1. What is the meaning of the word *running* in the phrase "running the government" on page 23? Is this a literal or a nonliteral meaning of the word?

   _____

   _____

2. If *running* has a literal meaning on page 23, what is a nonliteral meaning of the word? If *running* has a nonliteral meaning on page 23, what is a literal meaning of the word?

   _____

   _____

   _____

3. What is the meaning of the word *heard* as it is used in the phrase "other interests are heard" on page 25? Is this a literal or a nonliteral meaning of the word?

   _____

   _____

4. If *heard* has a literal meaning on page 25, what is a nonliteral meaning of the word? If *heard* has a nonliteral meaning on page 25, what is a literal meaning of the word?

   _____

   _____

   _____

Students analyze and respond to literary and informational text.

Name _____

Introduce the Topic Begin an introduction for an opinion essay that responds to the following question: *What, in your opinion, is the most important function of government?* First, read the different functions of government described on pages 4–9 of *What Is a Government?* Next, decide which of those functions is the most important. Then, think about introductions that caught your attention, and brainstorm ways to catch your readers' attention. Finally, introduce the topic of government in an interesting way in two or three sentences.

_____

_____

_____

_____

_____

_____

Conventions

Ensure Subject-Verb Agreement in Past Tense

DIRECTIONS Complete each sentence with the correct past-tense form of the verb *to be*.

1. My old school _____ down the street from my house.

2. The town's hospitals _____ all built within the last ten years.

3. You _____ happy to get a chance to see the play.

Students write routinely for a range of tasks, purposes, and audiences. Students practice various conventions of standard English.

Name _____

DIRECTIONS Write a sentence using each word.

participating   issue   protest   occupation

_____

_____

_____

_____

_____

Write in Response to Reading

Read pages 28–29 of *What Is a Government?* Write a paragraph describing an issue in your school and how you can make your feelings about the issue known. Use evidence from the text in your response.

_____

_____

_____

_____

_____

Students demonstrate contextual understanding of Benchmark Vocabulary. Students read text closely and use text evidence in their written answers.

Name _____

Text Features and Search Tools

DIRECTIONS Using evidence from the text, answer the following questions about pages 28–32 from *What Is a Government?*

1. What is the definition of *democracy* in the glossary?

_____

_____

2. What are the definitions of *parliament* and *president* in the glossary?

_____

_____

_____

_____

3. How do these three definitions make clear the similarities and differences between being a president and being a member of parliament in a democracy?

_____

_____

_____

_____

4. Based on information in the index, on which pages of the text could you find information to help you better understand the similarities and differences between being a president and being a member of parliament?

_____ _____

Students analyze and respond to literary and informational text.

Name _____

State an Opinion Write an opinion statement in response to the prompt from Lesson 4. First, reread the section of the text about the different functions of government on pages 4–9 of *What Is a Government?* Next, review your introduction from Lesson 4. Then, form an opinion about which function of government is most important. Finally, state your opinion, which may include a key fact or detail.

_____

_____

_____

_____

_____

Ensure Subject-Verb Agreement in Present Tense

DIRECTIONS Complete each sentence with the correct present-tense form of the verb *to write.*

1. I _____ a letter to my representative about the park near my house.

2. They _____ an e-mail to the mayor about city schools.

3. She _____ a letter to the editor of the local newspaper about recycling.

Students write routinely for a range of tasks, purposes, and audiences. Students practice various conventions of standard English.

Name _____

Final Syllables

DIRECTIONS Circle the correctly spelled word in each pair.

1. commosion   commotion
2. invasion   invation
3. generasion   generation
4. posision   position
5. relaxasion   relaxation
6. division   divition
7. vacasion   vacation
8. explotion   explosion

DIRECTIONS Add **-ture, -ive,** or **-ize** to complete each word below. Write the complete word on the line. There is only one correct choice for each word.

9. pas _____   13. maxim _____
10. act _____   14. real _____
11. rup _____   15. cap _____
12. mass _____   16. adven _____

DIRECTIONS Choose four words from the above list and write a sentence for each word.

17. _____

18. _____

19. _____

20. _____

Students apply grade-level phonics and word analysis skills.

Name _____

DIRECTIONS Write a sentence using each word.

inspired   influential

_____

_____

_____

_____

Write in Response to Reading

Read *What Is a Government?* Write a paragraph describing which ancient government you would have liked to live under. Use text evidence in your response.

_____

_____

_____

_____

_____

_____

Students demonstrate contextual understanding of Benchmark Vocabulary. Students read text closely and use text evidence in their written answers.

Name _____

Support an Opinion with Reasons Make a list of reasons that support your opinion about the most important function of government. First, review the descriptions on pages 4–9 of the text, your introduction from Lesson 4, and your opinion statement from Lesson 5. Then, list three reasons that support your opinion, and provide additional details for each reason, if available. Use the text to help you come up with reasons and details that support your opinion.

_____

_____

_____

_____

_____

_____

Conventions

Ensure Subject-Verb Agreement in Future Tense

DIRECTIONS Use the future-tense form of each verb below in a sentence.

1. vote _____.

2. lead _____.

3. control _____.

Students write routinely for a range of tasks, purposes, and audiences. Students practice various conventions of standard English.

Name _____

DIRECTIONS Write a sentence using each word.

centuries   merchant

_____

_____

_____

_____

Write in Response to Reading

Read page 84 from *Who Really Created Democracy?* Do you think the people of Athens had the right to be frustrated? Explain your answer using evidence from the text.

_____

_____

_____

_____

_____

Students demonstrate contextual understanding of Benchmark Vocabulary. Students read text closely and use text evidence in their written answers.

Name _____

Word Relationships

DIRECTIONS Using evidence from the text, answer the following questions about pages 83–85 from *Who Really Created Democracy?*

1. Find the word *debts* on page 83. What are debts?

_____

_____

2. Use the word *debts* in a sentence about something in real life.

_____

_____

3. On page 83, find the word *frustrated*. Why are the farmers frustrated?

_____

_____

4. Read page 85. Why would the colonists be frustrated?

_____

_____

_____

5. Use the word *frustrated* in a sentence about something in real life.

_____

_____

Students analyze and respond to literary and informational text.

Create an Organizational Structure Use the following steps to create a structure for your opinion piece:

1. On a separate sheet of paper, create a Web B graphic organizer with your opinion statement from Lesson 5 in the center circle.

2. Use your list of reasons from Lesson 6 to fill in the outer circles with reasons that support your opinion statement.

3. Add bullet points with additional details about the reasons.

4. Number the reasons in the order you will use them.

Then use the graphic organizer to write the first draft of your opinion piece on a separate sheet of paper.

Conventions

Identify Antecedents for Pronouns

DIRECTIONS Read the sentences. On the line, write which word is the antecedent for the underlined pronoun(s). Remember that more than one pronoun can refer to the same antecedent.

1. The wealthy lawmakers know <u>they</u> can't continue to fight the masses.

   _____

2. The king is furious. <u>He</u> is making harsher laws. _____

3. In a democracy, people—rich and poor—make laws together. <u>They</u> also choose <u>their</u> own leaders. _____

Students write routinely for a range of tasks, purposes, and audiences. Students practice various conventions of standard English.

Name _____

DIRECTIONS Write a sentence using each word.

aristocrat   unrest   trials

_____

_____

_____

_____

Write in Response to Reading

Read page 86 from *Who Really Created Democracy?* Write a paragraph about Solon's power in Athens. Support your writing by using text evidence.

_____

_____

_____

_____

_____

_____

Students demonstrate contextual understanding of Benchmark Vocabulary. Students read text closely and use text evidence in their written answers.

Name _____

Use Linking Words to Connect Ideas On a separate sheet of paper, rewrite your opinion essay, and use linking words and phrases to connect opinions and reasons. Refer to your Web B graphic organizer as a reminder of the organizational structure that shows how the reasons and details are related to your opinion. Then add linking words and phrases, such as *because*, *so*, *therefore*, and *as a result*, to your essay to connect your reasons to your opinions.

Conventions

Ensure Pronoun-Antecedent Agreement

DIRECTIONS Complete each sentence with a pronoun that agrees with the underlined noun or pronoun.

1. <u>Citizens</u> of Athens worried that _____ would have no power.

2. <u>Solon</u> loved _____ city and made important improvements to its government.

3. <u>Some</u> of the colonists were forced to let British soldiers stay in

   _____ homes.

Students write routinely for a range of tasks, purposes, and audiences. Students practice various conventions of standard English.

Name _____

DIRECTIONS Write a sentence using each word.

control   serve

_____

_____

_____

_____

Write in Response to Reading

Write an opinion paragraph about the ruler Hippias. How do you feel about his laws and policies? Support your writing by using text evidence.

_____

_____

_____

_____

_____

_____

Students demonstrate contextual understanding of Benchmark Vocabulary. Students read text closely and use text evidence in their written answers.

Provide a Concluding Statement Write a concluding statement for your opinion piece. Review the ideas for a concluding statement that you wrote in your Web B graphic organizer. Then choose the best idea and write a concluding statement, which can also be a question.

_____

_____

_____

_____

_____

Produce Simple Sentences

DIRECTIONS Read page 92 of *Who Really Created Democracy?* Write three simple sentences about Peisistratus.

1. _____

2. _____

3. _____

Students write routinely for a range of tasks, purposes, and audiences. Students practice various conventions of standard English.

Name _____

DIRECTIONS Write a sentence using each word.

council   judicial   executive   legislative   hurdles

_____

_____

_____

_____

_____

_____

Write in Response to Reading

Write an opinion paragraph about the author's point of view about who won the "race for democracy." Use text evidence to support your opinion.

_____

_____

_____

_____

_____

Students demonstrate contextual
understanding of Benchmark Vocabulary.
Students read text closely and use text
evidence in their written answers.

Name _____

Distinguish Points of View

DIRECTIONS Using evidence from the text, answer the following questions about pages 96–98 from *Who Really Created Democracy?*

1. What is the author's point of view about Cleisthenes? Explain your answer.

   _____

   _____

   _____

2. What is your point of view about Cleisthenes?

   _____

   _____

3. What is the author's point of view about the winner of the race to democracy? Explain your answer.

   _____

   _____

   _____

   _____

   _____

4. What is your point of view about the winner of the race to democracy?

   _____

   _____

   _____

Students analyze and respond to literary and informational text.

Name _____

Provide a Concluding Section Write a concluding section for your opinion piece. Refer to your Web B graphic organizer for ideas to include in your concluding section. As you think about how to bring your piece to a logical, satisfying ending, consider what final idea you want the reader to take away. Then write the concluding section for your opinion piece on the lines below.

_____

_____

_____

_____

_____

Conventions

Produce Compound Sentences

DIRECTIONS Combine each pair of sentences using *so, or, and,* or *but*.

1. The new government divides power. It gives people a voice.

_____

_____

2. The people of Athens were the first to form a democracy. They win the "race for democracy."

_____

_____

Students write routinely for a range of tasks, purposes, and audiences. Students practice various conventions of standard English.

Name _____

Prefixes *im-*, *in-*

DIRECTIONS For each definition, write a word on the line that begins
with *im-* or *in-*.

1. not mature _____

2. not complete _____

3. not sincere _____

4. not polite _____

5. not perfect _____

6. not movable _____

7. not dependent _____

8. not capable _____

9. not personal _____

10. not possible _____

11. not correct _____

12. not direct _____

13. not practical _____

14. not probable _____

15. not pure _____

DIRECTIONS Now write three sentences of your own. In each sentence,
include at least one of the *im-* or *in-* words from above.

16. _____

17. _____

18. _____

Students apply grade-level phonics and
word analysis skills.

Benchmark Vocabulary

Name _____

DIRECTIONS Write a sentence using each word.

representatives   candidate   aristocrat   unrest

_____

_____

_____

_____

_____

Write in Response to Reading

Skim *Who Really Created Democracy?* and *What Is a Government?* Select one of the texts, and write a paragraph explaining its main idea. Use text evidence in your response.

_____

_____

_____

_____

_____

Students demonstrate contextual understanding of Benchmark Vocabulary. Students read text closely and use text evidence in their written answers.

Name _____

Compare and Contrast

DIRECTIONS Using evidence from the texts, answer the following questions about *What Is a Government?* and *Who Really Created Democracy?*

1. What is one similarity between the ways *What Is a Government?* and *Who Really Created Democracy?* describe democracy?

_____

_____

_____

2. What is one difference between the ways *What Is a Government?* and *Who Really Created Democracy?* describe democracy?

_____

_____

_____

_____

3. What is one similarity between the ways *What Is a Government?* and *Who Really Created Democracy?* describe voting?

_____

_____

4. What is one difference between the ways *What Is a Government?* and *Who Really Created Democracy?* describe voting?

_____

_____

Students analyze and respond to literary and informational text.

Name _____

Gather Information to Build Knowledge Find print and digital sources on forms of government or individual rights. On the lines below, write the title of each source, the information each source can provide, and an explanation of why each source is reliable.

_____

_____

_____

_____

_____

Conventions

Define Complex Sentences

DIRECTIONS Underline the subordinate clause in each complex sentence. Circle the subordinating conjunction.

1. No laws are made in Athens unless they are approved by the Assembly.

2. The Americans actually studied Athens's ancient democracy when they designed their government.

3. After leaders debated many issues, they finally came to an agreement.

Students write routinely for a range of tasks, purposes, and audiences. Students practice various conventions of standard English.

Name _____

DIRECTIONS Write a sentence using each word.

cooperating   delegates   anxious

_____

_____

_____

_____

Write in Response to Reading

Read pages 100–101. Write a paragraph describing the events leading up to the start of the convention.

_____

_____

_____

_____

_____

Students demonstrate contextual understanding of Benchmark Vocabulary. Students read text closely and use text evidence in their written answers.

Main Idea and Details

DIRECTIONS Using evidence from the text, answer the following questions about pages 99–104 from *A More Perfect Union*.

1. After the revolution has ended, what problems does the United States face?

   _____

   _____

2. What do the leaders plan?

   _____

   _____

3. What is the main idea on pages 102–103? Which details on pages 102–103 support the main idea?

   _____

   _____

   _____

   _____

4. What is the main idea on page 104? Which details on page 104 support the main idea?

   _____

   _____

   _____

   _____

Students analyze and respond to literary and informational text.

Name _____

Take Brief Notes on Sources Take notes on key facts and details from pages 100–104 of *A More Perfect Union* on the lines below. Then, on a separate sheet of paper, write your notes in a T-Chart graphic organizer.

_____

_____

_____

_____

_____

_____

Simple, Compound, and Complex Sentences

DIRECTIONS Write whether the following sentences are simple, compound, or complex. Underline coordinating conjunctions and circle subordinating conjunctions.

1. I walked to school, and I was late. _____

2. My stomach hurts. _____

3. I am going to the game after I finish my homework. _____

Students write routinely for a range of tasks, purposes, and audiences. Students practice various conventions of standard English.

Name _____

DIRECTIONS Write a sentence using each word.

compromise   document

_____

_____

_____

Write in Response to Reading

Read page 109 of *A More Perfect Union*. After agreeing upon the Great Compromise, some delegates took a vacation while others continued working. Write a few sentences that explain why this happened.

_____

_____

_____

_____

_____

Students demonstrate contextual understanding of Benchmark Vocabulary. Students read text closely and use text evidence in their written answers.

Name _____

America's National Bird

In 1782, the American bald eagle became the symbol of the United States. It was chosen because it's a majestic and strong bird. How did this bird get chosen?

After the Declaration of Independence was signed in 1776, a committee was asked to research a symbol for our new country. This committee included Thomas Jefferson, John Adams, and Benjamin Franklin. They presented an illustration of a woman called "Liberty" holding a shield.

Congress wasn't impressed. It turned to a Philadelphia artist. The artist's design included a golden eagle. This species wasn't unique to the United States. After some research, Congress chose the American bald eagle. Today, the eagle is pictured on our country's seal, money, and on many stamps.

Not everyone liked this symbol. Benjamin Franklin shared his displeasure in a letter to his daughter in 1784. He said, "For my own part I wish the Bald Eagle had not been chosen the Representative of our Country. He is a Bird of bad moral Character." Franklin felt the American Bald Eagle stole food from other birds and was a coward.

However, Franklin was happy to see that the illustration of the eagle looked more like a turkey. He felt the turkey was a more appropriate symbol. Franklin believed the turkey was courageous in its own way.

Nevertheless, the American bald eagle still represents our country. President John F. Kennedy agreed with the Founding Fathers and once wrote, "The fierce beauty and proud independence of this great bird aptly symbolizes the strength and freedom of America."

Students read text closely to determine what the text says.

Name _____

Gather Evidence Circle details that Benjamin Franklin used in his argument against the American bald eagle as our country's national symbol.

Gather Evidence: Extend Your Ideas Write details that Benjamin Franklin used in his argument in favor of turkeys as our country's national symbol. Do you agree with his argument? Explain why in one to two sentences.

_____

_____

_____

Ask Questions You are on a committee to decide what mammal should be our country's symbol. Underline details from the article to support your decision.

Ask Questions: Extend Your Ideas What questions would you research to inform your decision? Write at least two questions.

_____

_____

Make Your Case Underline two pieces of information from the selection that you think could have been better explained with an illustration.

Make Your Case: Extend Your Ideas What do you think is the most interesting information you learned in this selection that is provided only by the images and not by the text? Explain.

_____

_____

Students read text closely to determine what the text says.

Name _____

Sort Evidence On a separate sheet of paper, rewrite notes from Lesson 12, sorting them into the following categories:

- People at the Convention
- Details About the Convention
- New Ideas
- Problems
- Solutions

Decide which facts and details from pages 100–104 belong in each category. Then add notes from pages 105–109 of *A More Perfect Union*.

Capitalize Appropriate Words in Titles

DIRECTIONS Write the titles using correct capitalization.

1. connecticut compromise _____

2. new jersey plan _____

3. declaration of independence _____

Students write routinely for a range of tasks, purposes, and audiences. Students practice various conventions of standard English.

Name _____

DIRECTIONS Write a sentence using each word.

unanimous   proposed

_____

_____

_____

_____

Write in Response to Reading

Explain the meaning of "the spirit of compromise" on page 110. Support your writing with text evidence.

_____

_____

_____

_____

_____

_____

Students demonstrate contextual understanding of Benchmark Vocabulary. Students read text closely and use text evidence in their written answers.

Name _____

Literal and Nonliteral Meanings

DIRECTIONS Using evidence from the text, answer the following questions about pages 110–119 from *A More Perfect Union*.

1. On page 111, the text says that some of the delegates "left the convention in anger." What does this phrase mean? Is it literal or nonliteral? Explain.

   _____

   _____

   _____

2. Read the following sentence from page 114: "Much hard work still lay ahead." Is this sentence literal or nonliteral? Explain your answer.

   _____

   _____

   _____

3. Explain the phrase "serve his country well" on page 116.

   _____

   _____

   _____

4. What is the meaning of the following phrase from page 115: "afraid the government would be too strong"?

   _____

   _____

   _____

Students analyze and respond to literary and informational text.

Name _____

Plan and Prewrite On the lines below or on a separate sheet of paper, write an outline for an opinion piece about forms of government or individual rights as presented in this unit. Use evidence from the texts in this unit to support your opinion. Use Roman numerals and lowercase letters to organize your reasons and evidence.

_____

_____

_____

_____

_____

Conventions

Define Adverbs

DIRECTIONS Circle the adverb in each sentence, and underline the word that the adverb modifies. Tell what information the adverb gives.

1. The new Congress began to work immediately.

_____

_____

2. Parchment is a very special kind of paper.

_____

_____

3. Others would have signed the document, but they went home early.

_____

_____

Students write routinely for a range of tasks, purposes, and audiences. Students practice various conventions of standard English.

Name _____

DIRECTIONS Write a sentence using each word.

cooperating   compromise

_____

_____

_____

_____

Write in Response to Reading

Read pages 104–108 of *A More Perfect Union*. Write a paragraph explaining why the delegates came up with the Connecticut Compromise.

_____

_____

_____

_____

_____

Students demonstrate contextual understanding of Benchmark Vocabulary. Students read text closely and use text evidence in their written answers.

Name _____

Historical Events

DIRECTIONS Using evidence from the text, answer the following questions about *A More Perfect Union*.

1. Why did the thirteen colonies fight the Revolutionary War?

   _____

   _____

2. Why did the members of the Committee of Detail not take a vacation?

   _____

   _____

   _____

3. Why didn't all the delegates sign the new Constitution?

   _____

   _____

   _____

4. Why was the Bill of Rights added to the Constitution?

   _____

   _____

   _____

Students analyze and respond to literary and informational text.

Writing

Draft Using the outline you wrote in Lesson 14, write a first draft of your opinion essay on forms of government or individual rights. Be sure to use evidence from the texts to support your opinion. Write your draft on a separate sheet of paper.

Conventions

Function of Adverbs

DIRECTIONS Write three sentences that include adverbs about the events described in *A More Perfect Union*. Underline the adverbs you use.

1. _____

   _____

2. _____

   _____

3. _____

   _____

Students write routinely for a range of tasks, purposes, and audiences. Students practice various conventions of standard English.

Name _____

Related Words

DIRECTIONS Choose the word that best matches each clue. Write the word on the line.

1. coverings for the body   cloth clothes   _____

2. a person who plays sports   athlete athletics   _____

3. a person's handwritten name   sign signature   _____

4. to wash   bath bathe   _____

5. the world of living things   natural nature   _____

DIRECTIONS Read each pair of related words. Underline the parts that are spelled the same but pronounced differently. Write a sentence using one of the words in each pair.

6. feel   felt   _____

7. keep   kept   _____

8. decision   decide   _____

9. mean   meant   _____

10. definition   define   _____

11. volcanic   volcano   _____

12. pleasant   please   _____

13. relative   relate   _____

14. sign   signal   _____

15. repetition   repeat   _____

Students apply grade-level phonics and word analysis skills.

Name _____

DIRECTIONS Write a sentence using each word.

absolute   exception   delegates   unanimous

_____

_____

_____

_____

_____

_____

Write a paragraph in which you compare and contrast the main ideas of *A More Perfect Union* and *What Is a Government?* Explain how key details support the main idea in each text.

_____

_____

_____

_____

_____

_____

Students demonstrate contextual understanding of Benchmark Vocabulary. Students read text closely and use text evidence in their written answers.

Name _____

Revise Revise the draft of the opinion essay you wrote in Lesson 15. Use the following steps to revise your essay:

1. Revise your work based on the peer feedback you have received.

2. Make sure you have clearly stated your opinion.

3. Make sure you have supported your opinion with reasons.

4. Make sure you have supported each reason with evidence from the text(s).

Write your revised draft on a separate sheet of paper.

Conventions

Function of Adverbs

DIRECTIONS Circle the adverb in each sentence. Then underline the word it modifies. On the line below the sentence, write whether it tells how, when, or where something happened.

1. Transportation systems help people easily move from place to place.

   _____

2. The bill soon became a law.

   _____

3. Delaware approved the new Constitution, and four other states quickly followed.

   _____

Students write routinely for a range of tasks, purposes, and audiences. Students practice various conventions of standard English.

Name _____

DIRECTIONS Write a sentence using each word.

aristocrat   council   anxious

_____

_____

_____

_____

Write in Response to Reading

Skim *A More Perfect Union* and *Who Really Created Democracy?* Write a paragraph comparing and contrasting the information they provide about the early history of the United States. Use evidence from both texts in your response.

_____

_____

_____

_____

_____

_____

Students demonstrate contextual understanding of Benchmark Vocabulary. Students read text closely and use text evidence in their written answers.

Name _____

Compare and Contrast

DIRECTIONS Using evidence from the texts, answer the following questions about *Who Really Created Democracy?* and *A More Perfect Union*.

1. How are the texts' descriptions of the colonists' experience under British rule similar?

   _____

   _____

2. How are the texts' descriptions of the colonists' experience under British rule different?

   _____

   _____

   _____

3. How are the texts' descriptions of the development of the American government similar?

   _____

   _____

   _____

4. How are the texts' descriptions of the development of the American government different?

   _____

   _____

   _____

Students analyze and respond to literary and informational text.

Name _____

Editing Edit the revised draft of your opinion essay from Lesson 16.
Correct spelling, capitalization, and punctuation errors. Then make sure
that you have varied your sentence structure. Finally, write an edited
version of your essay on a separate sheet of paper.

Comparative and Superlative Adverbs

DIRECTIONS Complete the following sentences with the comparative
or superlative form of the adverb in parentheses.

1. Modern governments include women _____ (often) than past
   governments.

2. Which Athenian worked _____ (hard) to bring democracy to
   Athens—Cleisthenes, Solon, or Peisistratus?

3. Some delegates arrived _____ (late) to Philadelphia than
   others.

Students write routinely for a range of
tasks, purposes, and audiences. Students
practice various conventions of standard
English.

Name _____

DIRECTIONS Write a sentence using each word.

expectations   consulted   legislative   judicial   executive   document

_____

_____

_____

_____

_____

_____

_____

Write in Response to Reading

Skim *What Is a Government?, Who Really Created Democracy?*, and *A More Perfect Union*. In your opinion, which author's point of view best reflects your own? Use specific examples from the texts to support your answer.

_____

_____

_____

_____

_____

_____

Students demonstrate contextual understanding of Benchmark Vocabulary. Students read text closely and use text evidence in their written answers.

Name _____

Publish and Present Determine how you would like to publish and present your opinion essay. Then write your plans for a presentation on the lines below.

_____

_____

_____

_____

_____

_____

Conventions

Comparative and Superlative Adverbs

DIRECTIONS On the lines below, write two sentences that use comparative adverbs and one sentence that uses a superlative adverb.

1. _____

   _____

2. _____

   _____

3. _____

   _____

Students write routinely for a range of tasks, purposes, and audiences. Students practice various conventions of standard English.